HEREFORD &
THE WYE VALLEY

In the Forest of Dean

HEREFORD &
THE WYE VALLEY

A Walker's Guide to The Malverns,
Herefordshire and the Forest of Dean

by

David Hinchliffe

CICERONE PRESS
Milnthorpe, Cumbria

British Cataloguing-in-Publication Data.
A catalogue record for this book is available from the British Library.

DEDICATION

To Laura and Matthew

ACKNOWLEDGEMENTS

I could not have written this book without the willing co-operation and encouragement of more people than I could ever have expected. I can only thank those listed below, and beg the forgiveness of those I have omitted.

Geoff Allen	}	Hereford and Worcester County Council
Mike Radford	}	
David Hughes		The National Trust
Paul Thomson		Hereford and Worcester County
Countryside Service		
Miss K.Bradbury		Curator, Hereford Cider Museum Trust
Rachel Chamberlain	}	Forestry Commission
Gordon Adam	}	
T.J.Epps		H.P.Bulmer Drinks Ltd
Tony Price		Hereford City Council

Also to Steve Yeardley for his drawings, Sue for her support and drawings, and to my walking companions.

Front cover: Kerne Bridge

CONTENTS

General Introduction 7

About this Guide 9

Herefordshire: Introduction 11

    The Walks 24

The Malvern Hills: Introduction 83

    The Walks 92

The Wye Valley: Introduction 112

    The Walks 120

The Forest of Dean: Introduction 171

    The Walks 179

APPENDICES

1. Longer Distance Paths 207

2. Public Transport 209

3. Useful Addresses 210

Useful Books 211

HEREFORDSHIRE, THE WYE VALLEY & THE FOREST OF DEAN

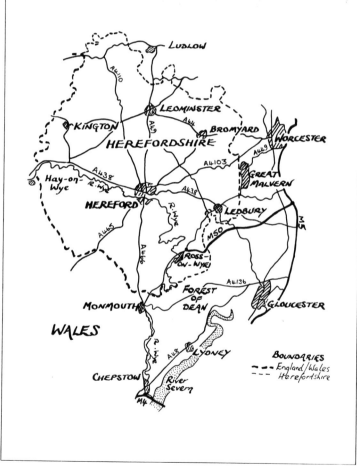

GENERAL INTRODUCTION

The writing of this book has been a rare privilege, for it has required the exploration of a beautiful and enticing tract of the British Isles. True, some of the walks in this book cover well-tramped paths, notably on the crest of the Malvern Hills and in parts of the Wye Valley. The surprise has been that only a short distance from these honeypots are lovely unspoilt areas which rarely see a rambler. I have tried to do justice to both the essential popular routes and those off the beaten track.

There are fifty-four walks in this book, but there could so easily have been many more without exhausting the storehouse of potential walking experiences. There is the opportunity to sample some of the exhilarating scenery here, where England rubs shoulders with Wales - this was not always a familiar and comfortable relationship. That it was a national frontier is often brought to mind by stern castle or ancient earthwork, or when one sees place names strangely alien to English eyes.

The variety of walking experience available should revive even the most jaded walking palate. Not all is as gentle and serene as it may at first seem, but few of the routes described require strenuous exertion or specialised skills. There are tremendous contrasts between the bleak ramparts of the Black Mountains and the friendly Malvern Hills, sheltering urbane and cultured Great Malvern, or between the plantations of the Mortimer Forest on the Shropshire border and the vast treescapes of the Forest of Dean. Pastoral and cultivated landscapes dotted with picturesque villages and farmsteads rest comfortably alongside these wilder areas.

There are common threads, notably the bewitching River Wye, which leaves Wales just outside the border town of Hay-on-Wye, wends eastwards, passes through Hereford, then trends south through a romantic gorge to join the Severn near Chepstow.

For convenience this book has been divided into four main parts, each with an introductory section. The County of Herefordshire, the Malvern Hills, the Wye Valley and the Forest of Dean each have their individual character yet blend one into the other without discord. They have beauty, are rich in wildlife and are often steeped in intriguing history. They share a benevolent climate and friendly people, yet are not over-run by tourism. They await your discovery.

Badger

ABOUT THIS GUIDE

The core of this book is the selection of fifty-four walks. Each contains a route description and a sketch map, plus additional information about the area and the sights to be seen. Each route description also provides details of the Ordnance Survey 1:25,000 map(s) covering the route. It is not necessary to buy all of these, but they can add to your understanding of the surrounding landscape. They are invaluable to those who wish to deviate from the route, to explore other paths and tracks, but otherwise the book alone should be sufficient for you to find your way.

For most people the following maps will provide adequate coverage, placing the walks into context and clearly showing all the minor roads, so important in finding the start point:

OS 1:50,000 Landranger 148, Presteigne and Hay-on-Wye

OS 1:50,000 Landranger 149, Hereford and Leominster

OS 1:50,000 Landranger 150, Worcester and The Malverns

OS 1:50,000 Landranger 161, Abergavenny and the Black Mountains

OS 1:25,000 Outdoor Leisure 14, Wye Valley and Forest of Dean

Some walks give optional variations, to shorten or extend the walk. Others are capable of being linked together (see Appendix 1). The aim is to provide a flexible guidebook, so that newcomers to the area can follow clear routes, but those more experienced can use the book for reference whilst devising their own routes.

The walks range in length from 2km (1^{1}/2m) to 23km (14^{1}/2m). Allow at least 1 hour for each 3km (2m), or longer if you wish to allow for leisurely pub stops or additional sightseeing. This is an area to stand and stare, not to plough on relentlessly.

The start point is usually at or near a convenient car parking spot, except in towns. Public transport details are given, where possible, although sometimes this involves an alternative start point and a somewhat longer walk. Places of refreshment are also given, although opening times will depend upon season and day of the week. Useful leaflets are also listed, and background reading material for those wishing to explore in more detail is given in the

Useful Books section.

For those who wish to delve a little deeper, each section is preceded by some background information about the area - geology and scenery, wildlife, history and any special aspects. I hope that these details will put the walks into context and enhance your interest.

Care has been taken only to include paths which are rights of way, so you need have no fear of trespass. Usually gates, stiles and waymarks make routefinding relatively straightforward. If you should find a path which has been obstructed, perhaps by growing crops, please report the offence to the appropriate County Council.

For most of these walks little is required by way of specialist equipment, other than stout footwear. In inclement weather waterproofs will obviously be advisable, and for longer walks a rucksack containing clothing needed in the event of a change in the weather. Food and drink should be carried.

Please respect the Country Code, causing no damage, closing gates and keeping dogs under control, but above all enjoy your walking. I am sure that you will!

Speckled wood butterfly

HEREFORDSHIRE

INTRODUCTION

In today's fast-moving, computerised, commercialised, pressurised society many people yearn for a return to some half-remembered Golden Age, with a slower pace of life and a gentler rate of change. Summers were warmer, civility was normal and chocolate box lid scenes were to be found around every corner. The reality is that for most people this image never really existed, but that does not prevent us from pursuing our rural idyll. In many parts of the country this pursuit has brought cars and coaches, hordes of visitors and imaginative ways of parting visitors from their money, either destroying what they seek or turning it into a pastiche. So far Herefordshire has escaped the worst of this disease. Without pandering to tourism it retains a timeless air, having neither discarded its past nor preserved it as a hermetic abstraction.

Of course, the county has been off the beaten track for much of its history. Its position and natural resources did not lend it to industrialisation, and its roads led only to sparsely populated mid-Wales. Heavy clay soils and an undulating landscape found no favour with modern farming methods on a grand scale. For these mercies the modern visitor should be thankful.

Today the county is bound in administrative union with Worcestershire, but this section is confined to the old boundaries. We find a county of some 218,078 hectares (842 sq m) and a population of only 147,000. The major centres are Hereford (49,000 residents), Leominster (9,000), Ross-on-Wye (8,500), Ledbury (5,000), Bromyard (3,000) and Kington (2,000). Although not densely populated, neither are there any great areas of wilderness - around every corner is a cottage, farm or hamlet. The landscape is lived-in, like a warm friendly overcoat, not bleak and barren.

The visitor today will find that despite town centre "improvements" most of the larger communities retain much of their original charm, and all bar Leominster (pronounced "Lemster") are visited by the following walks. Smaller villages tend to be even more delectable, with half-timbered cottages abounding in parts of the county.

Surrounding these communities is a rolling landscape with some fetching scene or curiosity at almost every turn. Although modern arable farming has encroached on more traditional areas, pastures with sheep and the distinctive Hereford cattle, hop yards and apple orchards are still reasonably plentiful. Thick hedgerows and woodlands make this a green landscape, especially when viewed from above.

The climate is particularly kind, being sheltered from extreme high winds and having a low rainfall.

If the countryside is sparsely populated and visitors, especially ramblers, are few in number, there must be a snag somewhere. There is. Once off the beaten track the footpath network so clearly delineated on Ordnance Survey maps is at best patchy and at worst non-existent. In some parishes the majority of definitive paths have all but vanished. Elsewhere in the country this may be due to wilful obstruction by landowners, but this is rarely the case in Herefordshire. More often paths have fallen into disuse, have become overgrown and are then forgotten. Rambler's groups, officers of the County Council and the Forestry Commission all do their best, but far more resources are required if any impact is to be made. More than this, the paths need to be regularly walked, particularly by local people.

Geology and Landscape

An understanding of the underlying geology can explain so much about an area - its topography, natural history, agriculture, settlements and buildings. So often the sheer complexity of geological maps with flamboyant colours, dip angles and fault lines can exasperate and frustrate the beginner. Herefordshire has a basic simplicity of geology, which suggests that this is a good place for the novice to start.

Virtually all the county's rolling hills and vales are formed of the Old Red Sandstone deposited around 300-400 million years ago. At this time the sea which had covered the area during the preceding Silurian era was being replaced by more estuarine and freshwater conditions. This resulted in red marls and sandstones with cornstone (concretionary limestone) beds being laid down.

The gently undulating lowlands of central Herefordshire are

largely underlain by the Downton Series, of which the Ledbury Group is the thickest element. It seems to have been deposited in deltaic mud flats which the sea occasionally overran. This resulted in a cycle of deposition, typically starting with a coarse sandstone containing siltstone pebbles and fossil fragments, followed by finer laminated sandstones and siltstones with many traces of burrowing animals. Finally came thick unbedded siltstones with calcareous nodules. It is the rocks of this group which have weathered to form the distinctive heavy red soils of this central region.

The Ditton Series follows. Starting with red siltstones, marls and sandstones with thin bands of cornstone, followed by 450 to 600 metres of red marls and sandstone with beds of conglomerate and thin calcareous layers passing laterally into limestones. Again, there are cycles, typical of deposition in deltaic floodplains. These rocks form the hilly ground drained by the River Monnow, Bromyard Downs and the caps of Dinmore and Garnons Hills.

It should not be thought that the relative uniformity of the underlying rocks has resulted in a monotonous landscape. To the west the more resistant elements of the Old Red Sandstone rear up into the stark outlines of the Black Mountains of Wales. In the north, especially just south of Ludlow, earth movements and the existence of older Silurian strata give rise to more dramatic scenery. The Nature Conservancy Council has established a geological trail through a cross-section of the Silurian rocks. This visits thirteen locations over a distance of about three kilometres just south of Ludlow. A detailed booklet, illustrating some of the many fossils to be found strewn around these exposures, can be acquired at Ludlow Tourist Information Centre. Elsewhere, variations in the durability of the Old Red Sandstone give rise to isolated hills such as Dinmore, just south of Leominster.

Silurian rocks also outcrop to the west of the Malvern Hills, and are dealt with in that section of the book. One of the most fascinating areas is that of the Woolhope Dome, covered in the Wye Valley section.

Glaciation does not seem to have been a major factor in determining the shape of the landscape, although on Merbach Hill (Walk A8) three metres of glacial drift was found in a quarry 275m up the hillside. One thing the ice did do was to divert the course of the River Teme. It probably used to flow from Leintwardine north via Clungunford and Sibdon Carwood, then through the valley from Craven Arms to Onibury. This route was blocked whilst the ice was melting, resulting in the flooding of the Vale of Wigmore, until the Teme Gorge was formed to create an alternative route to the south.

Other than the lovely River Wye, and perhaps the Lugg and Arrow, the rivers of central Herefordshire tend to be rather insignificant, often no more than streams during dry summers. Their vales, such as those of the Frome and the Leadon, can nevertheless be quite striking in parts, and they add an extra dimension to villages such as Eardisland (Walk A15).

Natural History and Agriculture

Although it is common to separate consideration of the wildlife of an area from farming, in a county such as Herefordshire the two are inextricably linked. The fate of the plants, woodlands, birds and animals are dependent upon the nature of the agricultural, horticultural and forestry operations being carried out. Here again, Herefordshire has been somewhat fortunate. The heavy red soils have not lent themselves to the intensive arable farming of the eastern counties, despite the remarkably clement climate.

The central lowlands around Leominster and the Hereford plain are broken only by low hills. Here the soil is loamy and close textured. Although much pastureland remains, conventional arable farming is more prevalent than in the past. The area is not heavily wooded and there has been some hedgerow removal. Once the stronghold of the mighty Hereford bull, these great red and white beef cattle began to be selected in the nineteenth century. They were exported extensively to the United States and later to South America. These lovely beasts are still commonly seen in the county, although most walkers will hope that they are separated from them by a hedge or sturdy fence.

The reputation and wealth of Leominster was built upon wool - specifically the short staple wool of the Ryeland sheep. Turned out to graze after the rye harvest, it had its origins during the heyday of the monasteries, but began to be crossed with larger breeds at the time of the Napoleonic wars. There has been a recent gradual recovery in numbers.

The south-eastern lowlands are blessed with a thinner and lighter soil, formed from the higher beds of the Old Red Sandstone. This is the area drained by the Wye, Arrow, Frome and Lugg, typified by mixed farming. Here two distinctive crops of old Herefordshire can still be found.

Hops

Hops were probably first cultivated in the county in the sixteenth century, during the period when the English were making the transition from drinking ale to beer. The requirements of at least 0.5m of loamy soil with a medium to heavy texture and a light rainfall are ideally met in the valleys of the Frome and Lugg, where growing is now concentrated. In 1835 1,722 hectares of hops were grown around Bromyard alone, but higher yields and a demand for lighter beers meant a decline to about 260 hectares by 1985.

The plant belongs to the hemp/cannabis family, and is a hardy, long-lived perennial requiring a means of support. In the early days this meant poles, and plenty of them, the product of coppiced woodland. One can still find Hop Pole Inns, but by the mid-nineteenth century wirework was taking over.

In the hop yards (as the fields are known) the barren poles and skeletal wirework are visible for much of the year - creating this structure is a skilled job, sometimes requiring the use of stilts. The growth of the plant is remarkable - from the bines being attached to a string in April it takes just ten weeks for them to reach the top wire, up to 5.5m from the ground. By the middle of July it is starting to come into burr.

Picking is generally during September. At one time this required an army of pickers, the railways facilitating their invasion from the Black Country and South Wales. Between the wars over 4,000 pickers descended on the village of Bishops Frome alone. They were housed in farm buildings, tents and purpose-built (but crude) barracks. Those days are still remembered with affection for their social life and camaraderie. As so often, mechanisation, particularly after the Second World War, reduced the need for casual labour. The bines are now cut and loaded into trailers, to be taken to a picking machine in the farmyard, whereas at one time they were handpicked in the fields.

Other than the hop yards themselves, the other reminders of this industry are the hop kilns, known to the Men of Kent as oast houses. Once upon a time the hops were spread out in a loft to dry naturally, but the advantages of drying by means of smokeless fires, fuelled by Wyre Forest coal, coke and later anthracite quickly became obvious. Early buildings are low, two-storied and with pitched roofs. By the 1830s round brick kilns fitted with cowls were being built. By the 1870s they had evolved to larger, square structures with full-length ridge ventilators.

Drying was an arduous skill in itself. Twenty-four-hour shift work was needed to maintain a constant temperature. After drying the hops are packed into "pockets", weighing about 76kg, for despatch and sale.

For the walker the spectre of verticillium wilt is raised at the gate to all hop yards. Whilst this fungal disease will not attack the innocent rambler, it is rightly feared as the scourge of the hop world. It can be transmitted through infected soils being carried on boots or wheels, and when discovered the infected plant and those surrounding it have to be grubbed up and destroyed.

Cider

Apple orchards can be found in various corners of the County, those of the Marcle Ridge being particularly fine examples. The clayey soil helps to retain the moisture. At one time most farms would have had a cider mill, and today examples can be seen displayed as features in farmyards. The apples were crushed in the mills, which were powered by horse or ox. Much of the juice was collected at this stage, the pulp then being wrapped in cloths, eight or ten such bundles forming a "cheese", which was then placed in a press. The harvest takes place between August and December, traditionally the juice fermented in casks whilst the dessicated pulp was fed to the livestock.

The names of the apples have their own magic - the gennet-moyle, leather coat, foxwhelp and gillyflower to name but a few. Although the industry has declined in size the country's largest cider maker (Bulmers) is based in Hereford. A museum of the cider industry stands nearby (Walk A20). Smaller-scale producers include

Westons of Much Marcle (also specialising in perries, made from pears), and other "farmhouse" creations.

Finally, there are the border uplands. Here we enter typical hill country, with sheep and cattle, and small fields with high hedges being superseded by coarser grazing and finally the bleak ridges as the Black Mountains are approached.

Prehistory and History

The oldest evidence of man's existence in the area comes from King Arthur's Cave in the Wye Valley. In Mesolithic times the county was probably sparsely populated by hunting families. Neolithic man arrived about 2250 BC, bringing a more settled way of life based on primitive agriculture and crop raising. One group came via the Usk Valley, getting as far as Dorstone in the Golden Valley. The remains of the tomb-chamber known as Arthur's Stone are visited on Walk A8. The main concentration of population was between the Black Mountains and the Wye.

The Bronze Age commenced around 1800 BC, evidence being provided by the later beaker type of drinking pot utilised. The Iron Age of 900 BC onwards gave rise to the familiar hillforts for which the county is nationally famous. They had a lengthy and permanent occupation, Credenhill near Hereford at almost 20 hectares being the largest. Populations were also quite large - Croft Ambrey (Walk A3) had between 500 and 900 occupants. This certainly gives the impression of a reasonably settled and well organised civilisation. Perhaps 30,000 people lived in the county, evidence of a prosperous and well-organised agricultural system.

All went well until the Romans arrived. Initially they occupied lowland England, but were driven to subdue more and more of the country to secure their frontiers. Ostorius Scapulus found himself pitted against a wily adversary in Caratacus, son of Cunobelinus, the Belgic king. Finally defeated in AD 51, Caratacus was taken to Rome, where his stately manner meant that his life was spared and he was given his freedom.

The tribes of the Silures and Ordovices made various incursions and were not finally defeated until about AD 75. Wales was never really settled, being part of the military zone, so Herefordshire was

17

a borderland even in those days, and evidence of its civilisation at that time is limited. A villa discovered at Bishopstone in 1812 is the largest known in the county. Most settlements were on the best land, around Kenchester, Leintwardine, Stretton Grandison and Weston-under-Penyard. There was a network of roads, perhaps the major one being Watling Street West, running from Wroxeter in the north, between Leintwardine and Clungunford, across the Wigmore Valley to Mortimer's Cross, and thence to Hereford and Monmouth. Another ran from Stretton Grandison to Hereford (where the Roman Road runs along the northern city limits) to Kenchester and Clifford, and so into Wales.

Kenchester (Magnis) is the only known walled town, with a small population of perhaps 500. Weston-under-Penyard (possibly the Roman Ariconium) is supposedly linked to the iron works of the Forest of Dean - nearby at Bishop's Wood, Kerne Bridge, 18,000 Roman coins were found in 1875, many of which can still be seen in Hereford City Museum.

The Romans had left Britain by AD 410, and we then have little information about the area until the seventh century. The extent of Saxon settlement can be gauged from villages with "ham" and "ton" suffixes. These are prevalent around the Vale of Wigmore, between the valley bottoms and the heights (eg. Kington), east of Leominster and south of Dinmore, down into the Woolhope Dome.

By the seventh century the area was part of Penda's Mercian kingdom. His sons were Christian converts, and it was in their time that the minster was founded at Leominster, although the religious centre later moved to Hereford. The most visible sign of Mercian power remaining is Offa's Dyke, built in the late eighth century after a succession of battles against the Welsh, including one at Hereford in 760. Full details of the Dyke are given in Appendix 1.

Offa endowed Hereford Cathedral in 793 after the murder of King Ethelbert at nearby Sutton Walls. The name of the city is believed to derive from the Old English for "army ford", emphasising its strategic importance as a crossing place of the Wye.

Herefordshire only became known as such in the reign of Canute (1017-1035). The time of Edward the Confessor was one of turmoil and invasions - in this area the Welsh were again the culprits. Edward had spent twenty-five years in Normandy, and placed Normans in positions of influence - these included Richard Fitz-Scrob at Richard's Castle (Walk A1). Sweyn and Harold Godwinson were successively Earls of Hereford. In 1051 they rebelled and were driven out of England. They returned in 1052, Harold reclaiming his father's Earldom of Essex before his fateful end at the Battle of Hastings.

The Normans left many tangible remains of their stay within the county in the form of castles and churches. The most complete churches are to be found at Castle Frome (with its exceptional font), Kilpeck and its remarkable door way and at Moccas. There are also outstanding fragments, such as the tympanum at Fownhope (Walk C4), the chancel arch and the foundations of the round nave at Garway (Walk A14) and the doorway columns at Ledbury (Walk A19).

The border nature of the area gave rise to a high incidence of castles, many of simple motte and bailey construction. The motte was an earthen mound topped by a wooden tower with a palisaded court around it, the bailey being the larger courtyard containing domestic offices such as stables, chapel and workshops. It was defended by a rampart, ditch and palisade.

Good examples of motte and bailey castles can be seen on Walks A1 (Richard's Castle) and A10 (Snodhill). Lesser ones can be visited at Lingen (Walk A5) and Weobley (Walk A11). They are best seen where the site was abandoned before being developed into more sophisticated stone structures.

Along the Welsh border the Norman warlords developed into the Marcher lords. They were masters of all they could conquer, and their very existence depended upon Welsh unrest. As early as 1088 they revolted against the Crown, and throughout their existence they were a necessary evil to the King. There were rebellions during the wars of Stephen and Matilda in the mid twelfth century, and repeated raids by the Welsh. During the Civil War of Simon de Montfort the rebel based his operations in Hereford until he was defeated at the Battle of Evesham in 1265.

By the end of the thirteenth century the capacity of the Welsh to mount sustained campaigns against the English had been virtually crushed, yet in 1321 the Marcher Lords revolted against King Edward II, having been incensed by his favouritism of Hugh le

Despenser. The King and Despenser were betrayed at the Abbey of Neath and the King's favourite was executed at High Town, Hereford. The King was murdered the following year at Berkeley Castle in Gloucestershire.

By 1401 the Welsh had a new hero in Owen Glendower, and many campaigns against him were mounted from Hereford before his final defeat in 1408. Later, during the Wars of the Roses, the north of the County supported Richard, Duke of York, whilst the south was for the King. At the Battle of Mortimer's Cross in 1461 victory went to the future Edward IV.

Military matters then took a back seat, and Henry VIII took time out from dissolving the monasteries to abolish the Marcher lordships in 1536. The impact of the Dissolution was perhaps less in the county than elsewhere, those affected being in Hereford, Leominster, Wigmore and Abbey Dore.

Herefordshire last took a prominent part on the national stage during the Civil War. The county's gentry were traditionally moderate, although Charles' calls for Ship Money stretched their loyalty to the limit. The Harleys' home at Brampton Bryan in the north of the county was an isolated Parliamentarian stronghold. Skirmishes ebbed and flowed, the Royalists ensconced in Hereford for some time, whilst Parliamentary forces raided from Gloucester. One notable skirmish took place in Ledbury in April 1645, with Prince Rupert victorious.

Charles arrived in Hereford five days after his defeat at Naseby in 1645 in an attempt to rally support, but soon only Goodrich remained in Royalist hands, to capitulate in 1646.

There was some industry in the county in the seventeenth century, but it was largely by-passed by the Industrial Revolution. This was largely due to its location and poor communications. The roads were appalling - even the advent of the turnpike trusts in the eighteenth century gave little relief. There were attempts to improve the navigability of the Wye, and also the Lugg to Leominster, although a later phase of canal building benefitted Ledbury in particular.

Coaching services in the nineteenth century improved things for passengers and the mail. At one stage Hereford was connected to London by five different services, with links to Bristol, Liverpool and Aberystwyth also. The railway from Shrewsbury to Hereford opened in 1854.

Today Herefordshire still lacks major industry. The motorway network just clips one corner of the county and most roads are comparatively lightly trafficked - even on Bank Holidays. Rail links from Birmingham to Hereford and on to South Wales and from Hereford to Shrewsbury remain in place. Most of us will hope that Herefordshire never becomes an industrial centre, and that the only significant natural resource it possesses remains its beautiful countryside.

Croft Castle Walk A3. (see p29)

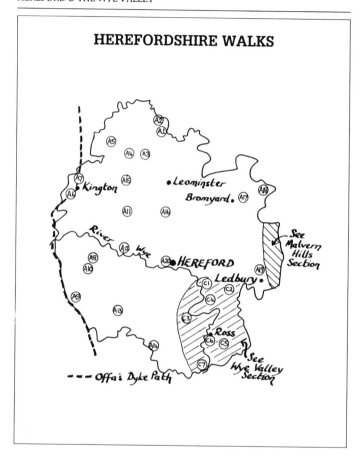

LIST OF WALKS

A1: RICHARD'S CASTLE AND HIGH VINNALS

                                         8.5km   5$\frac{1}{2}$m

A2: BRINGEWOOD FORGE AND DOWNTON CASTLE

                                          15.0km   9$\frac{1}{2}$m

A3: CROFT AMBREY   5.5km   3$\frac{1}{2}$m

A4: MERE HILL WOOD   7.0km   4$\frac{1}{2}$m

A5: HARLEY'S MOUNTAIN   9.0, 15.5   5$\frac{1}{2}$, 9$\frac{1}{2}$

                                         or 17.0km   or 10$\frac{1}{2}$m

A6: HERGEST RIDGE   9.5km   6m

A7: ON OFFA'S DYKE   9.5 or12.5km 6 or 8m

A8: MERBACH HILL AND ARTHUR'S STONE

                                          7.5km   5m

A9: THE CAT'S BACK   17.0km   10$\frac{1}{2}$m

A10: VAGAR HILL   9.5km   6m

A11: WEOBLEY   7.0km   4$\frac{1}{2}$m

A12: MONNINGTON WALK   6.5km   4m

A13: ABBEY DORE   13.0km   8m

A14: SKENFRITH, GROSMONT AND GARWAY

                                          23.0km   14$\frac{1}{2}$m

A15: PEMBRIDGE AND EARDISLAND 8.0km   5m

A16: WESTHOPE HILL   11.0km   7m

A17: BRINGSTY COMMON   5.5 to 9.5km 3$\frac{1}{2}$ to 6m

A18: BY RIVER TEME AND SAPEY BROOK

                                          15.5km   9$\frac{1}{2}$m

A19: LEDBURY AND WELLINGTON HEATH

                                          8.0km   5m

A20: HEREFORD CITY   6.0km   4m

Richard's Castle and High Vinnals

Distance:	8.5km (5$^{1}/_{2}$m)
Map:	OS 1:25,000 Pathfinder 951, Ludlow
Start Point:	Lay-by South of Overton on B4361, GR 498718
Public Transport:	None readily accessible
Refreshments:	None on route
Other Information:	*Mortimer Forest* leaflet, Forestry Commission *Guide to St Bartholomews Church and Richard's Castle*, from church (small charge)

Ludlow is a Shropshire town of great character, considered by many to be quintessentially English. Dominated by its castle, few guess that across the adjacent Herefordshire border is Richard's Castle, its ruined and remote status a poignant contrast to the stronghold of Ludlow. This walk gives an opportunity to visit Richard's Castle, on the way to the fine viewpoint of High Vinnals.

From the lay-by walk south, in the direction of Richard's Castle, until the aptly-named Black Pool is passed. Immediately on the right is a stile, leading briefly into a field, then into the wood. The path meanders along within about 20m of the woodland margin, initially amongst beech and ash, then oak and birch. Pass behind a few cottages, then bear left, out of the wood, along a track. At a junction of tracks leading to scattered cottages continue ahead down a grassy lane and through a gate.

Keep to the left, crossing at an opening into the field on the left, and follow the hedge until a stile leads onto a minor road. Go right to find the little community of Richard's Castle, where the church and the castle itself are signed to the right.

First in view is the church, its detached tower so placed to act as a lookout point for the castle without hindering its defence. Inside, remnants of ancient stained glass remain in the heads of some windows, and near the font is a thirteenth-century coffin lid with an

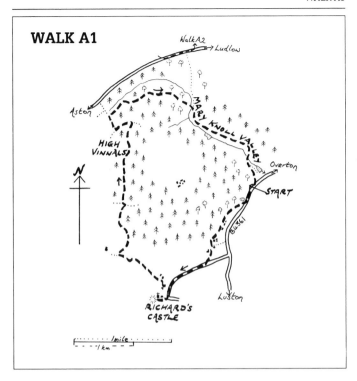

unusual raised pattern.

Now proceed through the churchyard gate to the castle. A few pathetic fragments of masonry remain, like rotting teeth in a gaunt smile which gives little inkling of its appearance in its prime. The earthworks are clear enough, and a perambulation in an anti-clockwise direction rises to the mound where the octagonal keep once stood. The steep drop to the west, although now well wooded, emphasises the defensive potential of the site. Continuing round, the decaying archway once formed part of the gatehouse.

The castle was founded in about 1050 by Richard le Scrob, a Norman favourite of Edward the Confessor, although he was less popular with the natives. The village, or small town, which grew up

25

outside the castle was probably defended by a town wall, and was originally known as Buiton or Boutanc. The castle appears to have fallen into disuse in the fifteenth century.

Retrace your steps as far as the road to the left, signed to Vallets, climb steadily and pass over a cattle grid, but turn right, just before the next grid. Enter woodland, and turn left upon joining a forestry track, then immediately right. The track is now guided by orange Forestry Commission waymarks, as it climbs easily to the summit of High Vinnals. Even without access to the lookout tower the views are superb. The radar station on Titterstone Clee is prominent, with the Malverns away to the south-west and the fastness of mid-Wales queuing up behind Bringewood.

Continue on the orange waymarked path, dropping quickly downhill, and going left on another path. Join a forestry track, the waymarks now orange, white and green. After another 100m take a track to the right, transferring allegiance from the orange to the green waymarks. You are now entering Sunny Dingle Woods, which in 1634 formed the setting for Milton's Mask of Comus, performed in Ludlow Castle. Butterflies are a speciality hereabouts - in late summer peacocks and silver-washed fritillaries, commas, ringlets and speckled woods vie for attention.

On the right hand side is a sign indicating a rock exposure, the fourth stop on the Mortimer Forest Geological Trail. The area was the first to be chosen by the Nature Conservancy Council as a geological trail. Most of the other stops are along the adjacent Ludlow to Wigmore road, illustrating the succession hereabouts. In this exposure can be seen the mudstones or fine siltstones of the Middle Elton Beds. Please do not remove samples from the face itself, but diligent searching of the ground below may reveal monograptids, orthoconic nautiloids and the trilobite Dalmanites.

When the opportunity presents itself, cross the stream and continue past Sunnydingle Cottage, then recross the stream. Pass through the forest gate, shortly after which a path forks to the right, looking down on a small lake before returning to the start point.

WALK A2:
Bringewood Forge and Downton Castle

Distance:	15km (9½m)
Map:	OS 1:25,000 Pathfinder 951, Ludlow
Start Point:	Along Deepwood Lane, between GR 482743 and 490744
Public Transport:	Alternative start from Bromfield, on Ludlow to Knighton bus route
Refreshments:	None on route

An opportunity to lose yourself in relatively unexplored countryside for the day. First across South Shropshire fields, then into Herefordshire along the River Teme at its best, with a glimpse of a trend-setting castle. Finally back through woodlands to complete a satisfyingly varied outing.

Take the stile by Woodcock Covert on Deepwood Lane, over the fields to a lane which joins a farm road. Go left, through the hamlet of Priors Halton, and continue past the mansion of Oakly Park. The road is now metalled, the house large and unprepossessing, but the ancient parkland here is attractive.

The River Teme is crossed in a scene of decay so advanced that it is now picturesque. On the right a weir and abandoned mills can be seen, whilst the bridge itself finds modern traffic almost too much to bear. Once safely over, a path is signed to the left, along the river bank. The field on the right is Crawl Meadow, so-called from the activities of a young lady intent upon marrying a knight. Her father so disapproved that he disinherited her, save for such land as she could crawl around in one night. Undaunted, she donned stout leather breeches and crawled round such a large area that her father repented. I suppose they must all have lived happily ever after.

The path curves to the right. Cross a track, then follow the field boundary to the right, to arrive at Lower Pool. Now go along the field boundary to the left to Stocking Nursery, where turn right. At the end of the wood there are stiles, then bear slightly left, gradually

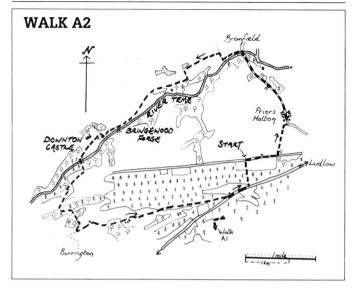

WALK A2

drawing closer to the Teme once more.

After this detour the route becomes a little clearer at a stile into the woods. The track may initially be somewhat overgrown, but press on to a bridge arching over the river, seemingly reflected in the semi-circular weir below. Continue along the river bank, past the derelict industrial buildings of Bringewood Forge. This is all that remains of the ironworks and community founded here in 1601.

Continue to a gate, and follow the track to the right. At the garage turn left and then cross a stile on the right to a terrace that passes below Downton Castle. The Castle was built between 1772 and 1778 by Richard Payne Knight, who also carried out much of the original design work. Although Pevsner describes him as a "virtuoso, archaeologist, anthropologist (in his way), prolific writer and bad poet", it has to be said that his architectural skills were quite impressive. Indeed, this is one of the earliest examples of the pseudo-medieval approach to the design of country mansions.

The grounds were laid out in the extreme picturesque style, with grottoes and the like, rather than the more restrained style of landscapers such as Capability Brown. Little remains in evidence as we cross the lively Teme for the last time, lingering long enough on Castle Bridge to gain a better view of the Castle than is possible from the terrace.

The track now wends its way past the lookout tower, over a stile and across a large field. Cross another stile and follow the track uphill, briefly left, then steadily right. Just as it levels out, and before it doubles back again, there is another stile into a field. Continue on the same line to enter the wood, plunging downhill to the left.

Yet another stile leads out of the wood from whence care must be taken with routefinding. Keep just left of straight ahead, cross a track in a belt of woodland, and make for a stile in the far left corner of the field. Down in the dip is a small footbridge; when safely over cross the next field to the far right hand corner. If all has gone well you will emerge on a rough road.

Go left, gradually gaining height as farms are passed. Re-enter Bringewood - if not exhausted there is a diversion left to a viewpoint, otherwise simply follow the forestry track to the road. Go left, and after about 100m, at the edge of the next tract of woodland, turn left on a path which falls swiftly downhill. Out of the woods, over a field, and you are back on Deepwood Lane, with the start point to the right.

WALK A3:
Croft Ambrey

Distance:	5.5km (3^{1}/$_{2}$m)
Map:	OS 1:25,000 Pathfinder 972, Tenbury Wells & Mortimers Cross
Start Point:	Croft Castle car park, GR 453656
Public Transport:	None
Refreshments:	None on route
Other Information:	National Trust guide to the castle and additional leaflets.
	Castle opens: April & October - Saturday &

Sunday, 2pm to 5pm. May to September - Wednesday to Sunday (and Bank Holiday Mondays), 2pm to 6pm

This is almost a case of castles ancient and modern. First visited is Croft Castle, dating from the fourteenth century, but a comparative newcomer when compared with the prehistoric fort of Croft Ambrey, which is seen later in the day. Although a short walk, parkland, woodland, fine views and a picturesque wooded valley can all be enjoyed.

Pass through the Gothik gateway to the castle. By all means visit the interior of the castle whilst your feet are still clean, otherwise go left immediately before the gateway. Opening hours are given above.

The Crofts, or de Crofts, were probably a Norman family who came to this country before the Conquest. They lived at Croft Castle from the Middle Ages (perhaps even earlier) until they sold the estate in 1746. Unusually they returned to the ancestral home in

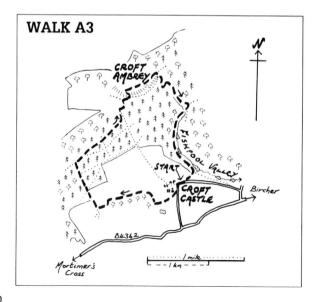

WALK A3

1923, and now Lord Croft is in residence, although the property has been in the ownership of the National Trust since 1957.

The original castle, dating from the fourteenth or fifteenth century, was given a less overtly military appearance in the eighteenth century. The most notable change was the creation of the Gothik bays which flank the main entrance, but the porch was a 1913 replacement, part of a programme which removed or amended some of the rococo Gothik work with plainer Jacobean. The interior was also transformed during the eighteenth century, the ceilings, panelling and plasterwork being especially fine. The "Strawberry Hill" decor of the staircase contrasts with the Georgian restraint of the dining room.

The church, of similar date to the house, lies within the castle grounds. It is distinguished by a lead-clad ogee cap to the seventeenth-century bell turret. Inside is an altar tomb to Sir Richard Croft and his wife. This knight captured the Prince of Wales at the Battle of Tewkesbury in 1471, having previously fought on the winning side at Mortimer's Cross a decade earlier.

Return towards the gatehouse and follow the edge of the ha-ha to the right. Pass through a gate and swing across the parkland, almost to the waterfowl-laden pond. Now tend to the right, towards some gnarled sweet chestnut trees, through a gate, and then to the left, along the single line of sweet chestnuts. This runs almost parallel to the recently planted lime tree avenue.

The sweet chestnut avenue runs for the next half mile. Stately would probably not be quite the right word for these 350 year old specimens. Huge and impressive certainly, but frequently contorted into living replicas of nightmarish illustrations in *Grimms Fairy Tales*. The Romans originally introduced these trees into this country, but unfortunately their edible nuts do not fruit as successfully over here as in warmer climes. Legend has it that the seed for these particular trees came from Spanish galleons wrecked on the Welsh coast. Unfortunately the danger of falling branches and treatment of diseased trees means that the avenue has had to be fenced off, the path running alongside it.

Continue over a stile and turn left then right, along the fieldside. Over another stile, then immediately right, before plunging into the wood ahead. At first the path is faint and overhung by low branches, but proceed boldly and you will soon arrive at a forest track. Cross over and head uphill along a grassy woodland ride. In these woods you may be fortunate enough to see fallow deer, or even the rare polecat.

At the top of the slope follow the track to the right, bearing left at the next junction and left again at the next but one to arrive at the south-western corner of Croft Ambrey fort. Follow the fence to a stile, then clamber over the earthworks to the left, taking the best route to avoid erosion to the highest part of the fortifications. The area has been excavated, suggesting that the site was occupied for about 600 years before the Roman invasion and that at its peak around 300 small dwellings were present. Some relics may be seen in Hereford City Museum.

Continue eastwards along the ramparts, the fine views marred only by the quarry of Leinthall Earls. Over a stile and then through a gate on the right, initially following splodges of blue paint on the trees, to enter Fishpool Valley. On the higher slopes adders may be found - please leave them alone. Lower down, in damper areas, grass snakes and slow worms occur. Common water birds on the pools are sometimes joined by a kingfisher, and the pied flycatcher may be spied. Needless to say, the pools also harbour dragonflies.

Either follow the path to the road, where turn right, or take an earlier path to the right, waymarked red and green, to return directly to the car park.

WALK A4:

Mere Hill Wood

Distance:	7km (4¹/₂m)
Map:	OS 1:25,000 Pathfinder 972, Tenbury Wells & Mortimers Cross
Start Point:	By the River Lugg at Aymestry (side of Crown Inn), GR 425654
Refreshments:	The Crown Inn, Aymestry
Public Transport:	Leominster/Leintwardine bus route

Aymestry

Eardisland

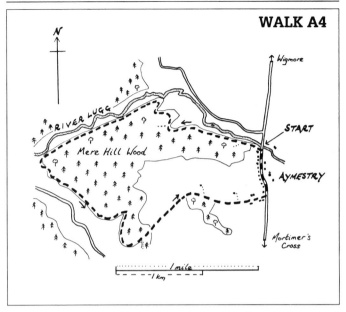

Long ago, at the end of the Ice Age, the swollen River Lugg carved a new channel through the North Herefordshire hills. The scars are long since healed and hidden by woods, but it is possible to follow this serene valley, and that abandoned those many years ago, with a return across more open uplands, and that is the route taken by this walk.

A good track sets off from the bridge into the woods. Soon limestone crags tower on the left. The valley was created when the previously south-flowing Lugg found its way blocked and, swollen by glacial meltwater, carved this new channel. A path to the left offers the opportunity to detour to a quarry face where the Aymestry limestone can be seen to good effect.

Returning to the main track, the deciduous woodland is left for the ubiquitous conifers, in this case largely Douglas Fir. Go left at a fork to find the track taking a wide detour, after which fork right. The river has been forgotten for a while, but now makes a welcome

Church Lane, Ledbury, Walk A19

reappearance, meandering alongside the track.

Finally the river parts company as the track arrives at a gate. Bear left, immediately below the small quarries, and climb to another gate to re-enter the woodland. This track closely follows the woodland margin, overlooking the Covenhope Valley, along which the Lugg once flowed.

The forest boundary has two indentations. At the apex of the second one a path scrambles up to the left, before striking off across country. Keep the field edge initially on your left, pass through a gate with the edge now on the right. The right of way is invisible underfoot, but bears to the left of Broad Leasow Wood, all the while with open views of the lowlands around Leominster.

Follow the edge of the wood to a lane, which descends to the road (the right of way across the fields to the Crown Inn was impassable at the time of writing). At the road go left, passing the church of Saint John and Saint Alkmund. The outstanding features of this church are the sixteenth-century screens, the linenfold panelling on the rood screen being particularly fine.

Continue along the road to return to the Crown Inn.

WALK A5:
Harley's Mountain

Distance:	9km (5¹/₂m), 15.5km (9¹/₂m) or 17km (10¹/₂m)
Map:	OS 1:25,000 Pathfinder 971, Presteigne
Start Point:	Lingen church car park (if no service) GR 365673
Public Transport:	Nearest bus service is to Presteigne
Refreshments:	The Royal George, Lingen

In the north-west frontier country of Herefordshire lies Harley's Mountain. No snow-capped peak this, just one unassuming hill amongst many, but the highest point on a lengthy journey through this relatively unvisited corner of the world. Even finding the start point can be a test of character and map-reading, but the reward is

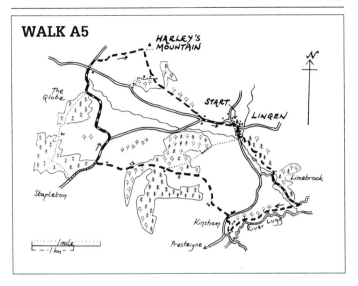

WALK A5

HARLEY'S MOUNTAIN

The Globe

START

LINGEN

Limebrook

Stapleton

Kinsham

River Lugg

Prestiegne

1 mile
- 1 km -

in the unspoilt hills, valleys and woodlands.

From the church car park walk into the churchyard. On the left is a stile, giving access to the motte and bailey of the old castle. Return to the churchyard - St Michael's was heavily restored following a fire in the nineteenth century and some pews still bear the scorch marks. Proceed down the main pathway to the road, where go left.

Round the corner a typically precise old AA plaque advises that it is $152\frac{1}{4}$ miles to London from The Royal George, here in the centre of Lingen. Of more immediate interest to many ramblers will be the modern invitation to sample Willie's Barley Beer. Pause to think that in the seventeenth century the village was the centre of a thriving pottery industry.

Take the path left, just before Brook House, to enter a field, where bear right. A sequence of wooden footbridges leads to a path along the woodland margin. Immediately after passing above Lingen Hall take a path (right) to descend to a track, then right again to emerge above the old mill at Limebrook.

Go right and pass through the yard to join a minor road. Now turn left, and at the roadside will be seen the few remaining fragments of Limebrook Priory, a nunnery founded at the end of the thirteenth century.

Continue along the minor road, until at a sharp left bend we go right, over our companion to date, the Lime Brook, to a gate. Bear left, along the base of the slope, to join the River Lugg - a name that scarcely does justice to this lovely river. This stretch of valley was created when the old course of the Lugg was blocked during the last Ice Age, and following the creation of a lake the water cut its way through this new route. It is allegedly the scene of a massacre of soldiers attempting to escape after the battle of Mortimers Cross in 1461.

Enter woodland, following the river, but after joining a metalled road watch out for a path on the right, leading up through the woods. At the top of the rise a little path on the right leads to Kinsham church, thought to have been built in the late thirteenth century, at the time of Limebrook Priory.

Return to the main path and go right, then left down the drive of Kinsham Court. Lord Byron rented the house in 1812/13 - some say he wrote Childe Harold here. Florence Nightingale also lived here during part of her childhood. The Arkwrights, of Spinning Jenny fame, moved here in 1910.

Turn right along the minor road, then take the farm track on the left. Now forget about routefinding for a while and just enjoy the views. The track climbs towards Cadwell Farm, and as altitude is gained more can be seen of the Welsh hills and the more heavily wooded slopes of Herefordshire and Shropshire.

Eventually the track descends through woodland and over a field to Noisy Hall - a modest and remote habitation which rests in bucolic silence until the unwary rambler disturbs the guard dog. Those already seeking mercy can go right, along a track. Continue ahead when this bends right, to cross two fields, re-enter woodland, and then head down a sunken lane. This emerges by the Baptist Church in Lingen.

The longer routes bear left through the wood into open countryside to join a minor road. Again a choice. To the left is the longest option, tough in places. An easier way is simply to follow the road to the right, meeting the longest route outside The Globe

Wood.

If you are determined to undertake the full walk go left, down to the hamlet of Stapleton, with the small Welsh border town of Presteigne in view ahead. Stapleton Castle is seen on a mound to the left. Appearances are deceptive as the masonry visible is that of a seventeenth-century house built on the site.

Immediately after a sharp right hand bend a path will be seen, leading off to the right. Follow this to enter Stapleton Wood, where waymarks guide you across a stream and steadily uphill. Exit the wood, and keep between the farm buildings and a muddy pond at Willey Hall. Descend diagonally across a field to a stile giving access to The Globe, another Forestry Commission plantation. A short climb leads to a track, where go left through spruce and larch trees to join a road.

Go left, and after a crossroads watch for a gate on the right. Pass through and along a gradually rising track, once more with the views over this border countryside improving as height is gained. Ahead and on the left appears the triangulation column at the summit of Harley's Mountain, but, alas, to conquer it (at 386m) would require an act of trespass. Incidentally, the Harley family were one-time landowners whose possessions included nearby Brampton Bryan, where the legendary Lady Brilliana resisted a lengthy siege during the Civil War.

Before drawing abreast of the triangulation column take a rather overgrown track on the right and descend to Red House. Cross the road, pass to the right of an out building, and then keep to the left and above a deepening valley. A sharp left turn at the field edge will soon lead you into Gullet Wood.

Go downhill and over a little stream. To the left is Clay Vallet Wood, part of which is a Herefordshire Nature Trust reserve. Now follow the field side. The bank on the right is smothered in primroses during early spring. Arriving in due course at the road go left and at a left-hand bend enter the field ahead. Continue ahead to regain the road with the church to your left.

WALK A6:

Hergest Ridge

Distance:	9.5km (6m)
Map:	OS 1:25,000 Pathfinder 993, Kington
Start Point:	Ridgebourne Road GR 284567. Park tidily on grass verge
Refreshments:	None on route, but pubs and cafes in Kington
Public Transport:	Kington has reasonable bus connections with Hereford and less frequent services to Hay-on-Wye, Leominster and even Aberystwyth and Llandrindod Wells

Some names evoke visions and inspire people from childhood - Xanadu, Samarkand and Timbuctu might fall into this category. For the domestic walker Striding Edge on Helvellyn often proves to have such magnetic attraction. When a hill on the Welsh border inspires a piece of music and has a name reminiscent of ancient heroes such as Hengist and Horsa, curiosity just has to be satisfied. If Hergest Ridge is no craggy, mystical place, it still provides an exceedingly pleasant walk.

The Ridgebourne Road climbs steadily past Hergest Croft gardens (open to the public from mid-April to late October), renowned for their azaleas and rhododendrons. In the hedgerows less spectacular common and uncommon plants may be found - these include the winter heliotrope, whose bright green circular leaves cover large areas in the spring, to be followed by long-stemmed flowers with a vanilla scent.

Passing through a gate we come upon the open hillside, climbing the convex slope. Alfred Wainwright, in his Pictorial Guides to the Lake District, describes such slopes as great deceivers, because they make it appear that the summit is just over the next rise - which it rarely is. Despite this the old racecourse is soon crossed, with most of the day's climbing now over. It is difficult to imagine that these

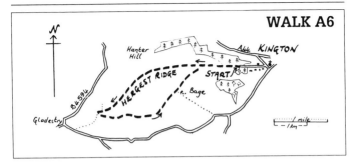

WALK A6

N

Hanter Hill

KINGTON

HERGEST RIDGE

START

Bage

B4594

Gladestry

1 mile
1 km

wind-swept wastes were once packed with cheering crowds and sweating horses.

Soon another curiosity comes into sight, a clump of monkey puzzle trees. No puzzles with the route, which curves round to the highest part of the ridge. Surprisingly, the triangulation column is at a lower height.

The path now starts to descend, with fine views to the hills of old Radnorshire. Just before the last knobble on the ridge, turn left on to a grassy track - the more obvious track slithers rapidly downhill, so don't be misled.

This grassy trod initially follows the field boundary, but maintains its height where the enclosures have not penetrated so far. The path dips into Rabber Dingle, then traverses gorse thickets, often with buzzards mewing over-head. There is one more dip, just before Bage Farm, before the outward route is rejoined. Turn right to return to the start point.

Buzzard

WALK A7:

On Offa's Dyke

Distance:	9.5km (6m) or 12.5km (8m)
Map:	OS 1:25,000 Pathfinder 993, Kington
Start Point:	Kington car park (off Mill Street)
Refreshments:	Ample choice in Kington
Public Transport:	See Walk A6

A number of walks in this book touch upon the Offa's Dyke Long Distance Footpath, but even where this coincides with remnants of the Dyke itself it is often half-hidden and gives little hint of its former stature. On this walk a clear section is seen, high on Rushock Hill, which might stir the imagination.

Kington - was it mighty King Offa, the Dyke-builder himself after whom this typically bustling border town was named? Muse upon this whilst leaving the car park by an alleyway, and turning right towards the Market Hall. Go left and walk up Church Street, turning right into The Square, now the terminus for local bus services. The road curves left before dropping down to Crooked Well, over Back Brook, and thence across the busy by-pass.

Follow the lane opposite, and watch out for the acorn sign on the right which indicates the path to the right of Rhue Villa. A path now leads to Bradnor Green. A sign points out the path which shortly passes over the golf links. This seems to be an "interesting" course, the highest in England or Wales, which might give even the golfing giants some food for thought.

Over a cattle grid and down a lane to the left of a farmhouse lies our route. Continue ahead, to the left of a belt of woodland, and then bear slightly left to stiles, now aiming left of the wood in the valley. There is another stile in the valley bottom, the direction now changing from north-westerly to north-easterly as height is gained. The path follows the field boundary, but where the hedge bends right we go half left.

On the horizon to the right can be seen three yew trees, two full-

grown and one still young, known as the Three Shepherds. The originals were planted over 200 years ago.

You will soon arrive at Offa's Dyke itself, where turn left. The rampart and ditch would have been much more substantial when first built, but the location alone is impressive enough. Reminiscent of Hadrian's Wall, striding away over the uplands amidst wagtails and wheatears, this is grand walking country.

The Dyke bends sharply to the left, with views to Stanner Rocks and Hanter Hill. All too soon height is lost as the Dyke is left behind. Our route curves past woodland to the col below Hanter Hill. Shortcutters can now bear downhill to the left, towards Holywell Farm. The longer route heads north with views down the valley of the Hindwell Brook, before trending left. Ignore the Offa's Dyke Path sign to the right by Lower Harpton Farm. Turn left onto a green track at the point where the main track goes right. Go through a gateway and then turn sharply right. The path deteriorates - this always makes even experienced walkers wonder whether they have lost their way, but it later improves.

In due course a gate is seen ahead. Do not pass through but go left, then right and right again, around the outside of a field, meeting those taking the shortcut on the way. On the right is a gate, which enter, alongside the ruins of Holywell Farm. Even traces of the well itself have all but vanished. The path now parallels the stream, until a bridge immediately before the farmstead of Dunfield. Instead of crossing the bridge, bear left (the path again indistinct) to a stile onto a path. Follow this through the woodland to the right.

Cross an open field to enter Bradnor Wood, where take the track to the left, uphill. The Forestry Commission has kindly provided sporadic footprint waymarks, which lead out of the wood, behind Dingle Cottage. Turn right for a few yards, and at the gable of the cottage go left, across the open hillside (no path). A new track is joined, leading past a new house. Immediately afterwards follow the field boundary to the right to join another track. Now go left, but where the track bends to the right continue ahead, passing between two barns before dropping down to the bypass.

Cross the road, go over a bridge and up the hill. Continue almost to the top, where go left to pass through the churchyard. The church tower dating from around AD 1200 was originally detached from the main body of the church, like so many others in the county. The spire is distinctive, described by Pevsner as being based on two truncated pyramids. Much of the rest of the church is of the thirteenth and fourteenth centuries, although there is a Norman font.

From the churchyard continue down Church Street to return to the town centre. By the way, Kington is supposedly named from Edward the Confessor, a hardly less notable attribution than Offa himself.

WALK A8:
Merbach Hill and Arthur's Stone

Distance:	7.5km (5m)
Map:	OS 1:25,000 Pathfinder 1016, Hay-on-Wye
Start Point:	Market Square, Dorstone, GR 313417
Refreshments:	The Pandy Inn, Dorstone
Public Transport:	Dorstone is on the Hereford/Hay/Brecon bus route

Dorstone and Bredwardine are two beautifully maintained and interesting villages straddling the ridge which divides the Golden Valley from the Wye Valley. The ridge contains the oldest man-made structure in Herefordshire, and is terminated by an outstanding viewpoint. This route makes the best use of a very neglected path network, its only defect being rather more road walking than is ideal. The roads are quiet, and the interest so great, that this is soon forgotten.

Start from the Market Square in Dorstone, a picturesque spot, although many years have passed since it saw a market. The village hall used to be a school, dating from the early seventeenth century. Nearby, the Pandy Inn reputedly originated in 1185, when Richard de Brito had it built to minister to the needs of those working on his new church. On the village green itself is the old cross, converted to a sundial in 1812.

Leave the square (actually a triangle) by the No Through Road to the church. Richard de Brito, one of the murderers of Thomas à Beckett, spent fifteen years in the Holy Land as a penance. Upon his return he established Dorstone church which was heavily restored in 1889. Our path keeps to the left of the churchyard, to cross the main road and enter the playing fields by a kissing gate to the right.

Bear slightly left to a stile, and then to a footbridge hidden amongst the hedgerow. This leads on to the trackbed of the former Golden Valley railway. Carry on to the far left-hand corner of the field where there is a stile and then some steps, here on overgrown

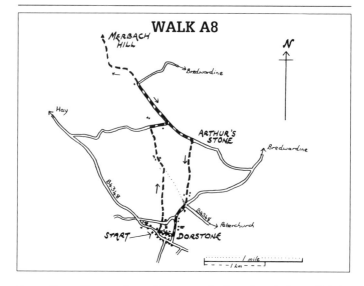

WALK A8

Merbach Hill

Bredwardine

Hay

ARTHUR'S STONE

Bredwardine

B4348

B4348

Peterchurch

START — DORSTONE

/ mile

— — — / km — — —

N

Spoon Lane. Emerge, hopefully unscathed, and again bear slightly left to a tarmac track, where go left.

The track climbs between the buildings of Wen Farm on its way to the road, where turn right. At the top of the hill go left. The road takes a 90° turn, but we pass through the gate ahead and initially follow the wall on the left, then keep to the height of the land, through a gate, to the summit of Merbach Hill. The triangulation column is at a height of 318m (1,043ft) amidst evidence of much former quarrying. It is said that eleven counties can be seen from here on a clear day. One seems to look straight down on the Wye as it wends its way from Hay to Hereford. Around can be seen Hay Bluff and Twmpa, the Radnorshire Forest and Titterstone Clee, to name but a few.

Return along the same path and the remarkably straight road, this time ignoring the road junction. Soon, at the side of the road, is the unmistakable crouching profile of Arthur's Stone. It is the stone skeleton of a communal burial chamber, originally covered by a 29m mound with a curved entrance passage. Constructed in Neolithic times, about 4,000 years ago, it was used for the burial of tribal chieftains.

At the rear of the enclosure a footpath sign indicates the return route, over a field. This follows the fieldside through a sequence of gates until at a choice of gates the right-hand one should be taken. This path descends towards a new house, and curves to the road, where go briefly left, then right, towards Dorstone. Take care on the blind bend.

At the next junction carry on in to the village and take the first right to return to the start point. A path by the village hall gives access to the motte and bailey remains of the former castle.

WALK A9:
The Cat's Back

Distance:	17km (10¹/₂m)
Map:	OS 1:25,000 Pathfinder 1039, Golden Valley
Start Point:	Black Hill picnic site, GR 288327. From Longtown follow Llanveynoe signs. Site is coyly signed 6km N of Longtown
Refreshments:	None on route. Pub in Longtown
Public Transport:	Bus services (one day per week) from Hereford via Abbeydore to Longtown. Halts at Cwm Steps near Llanveynoe
Other Information:	*On The Black Hill* by Bruce Chatwin is a work of fiction set locally

Of all the walks in this book, this is the one that closest approaches real mountaineering. The Cat's Back is a rocky ridge - perhaps no Striding Edge or Crib Goch - but unusual enough in this part of the world. The walk continues to Hay Bluff, at a height of 677m - over 2,000ft, before following the Offa's Dyke Path southwards on a broad peaty ridge. A walk for a fine, sunny day, to stride on enjoying the ever-changing views, without worrying about bulls, guard dogs, barbed wire - or even stiles!

From the picnic site go over the one and only stile on this walk,

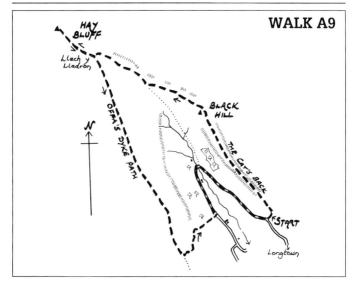

and climb the well-defined path up the open hillside. Soon the rocky outcrops that form the knobbly spine of the ridge, and which give it its name, become evident. A look back to the Skirrid and across to the white radar dishes of the satellite tracking station at Madley provide an excuse for a justified pause.

The path now climbs more steadily, and the ground levels out as the triangulation column of the Black Hill is approached. At 640m most of the day's exertion is already over. To the right the valley is that of the infant River Monnow, which flows to join the Wye at Monmouth.

The path soon swings away from the edge, and is joined by a narrow trackway that runs towards the Olchon Valley. Head for the prow of Llech y Lladron, before turning to the triangulation column on Hay Bluff at 677m (2,221ft). The column is mounted on a plinth which makes a convenient viewing platform. To the north, and over Hay-on-Wye, lies the undulating Welsh borderland, whilst to the east the Malverns can be seen on a clear day. Closer to hand the view ranges from Waun Fach, the headland of Twmpa, and the distinctive profile of Pen-y-Fan in the distance.

It is now time to retrace our steps, but this time continue over the rise of Llech y Lladron along the broad Offa's Dyke path, here peaty and slippery in wet weather, the heather prominent alongside. The transition to the drier grass slopes is noticeable. The next 5km (3¹/₂m) can be tedious if the weather is wet and visibility poor, but on a clear day it is sheer enjoyment to stride along the unobstructed ridge. The perspective of the distant views change, and one's only companions are the ubiquitous sheep and meadow pipits flitting around.

Along the way occasional clusters of gaudily painted boulders may be seen, a striking contrast to the generally sombre colours all around. To weary legs they may signal an escape to the valley below, but these Jezebels should be ignored, as so often they only flatter to deceive. Only at the official signpost to Dyffryn Olchon is it safe to turn left and zig zag downwards.

Go left upon reaching the minor road in the Olchon Valley. You will be unlucky if more than one vehicle passes you in the next 45 minutes, but determined short-cutters can take the green lane to the right after about 350m. There is a stream to cross and a steep climb, so it is easier just to follow the road, a typical country lane, alive with flowers in the spring and hung with hedgerow fruits in mellow autumn.

The Olchon Brook is crossed by bridge or ford (for those with dirty boots). Continue until the picnic site sign again appears.

WALK A10:
Vagar Hill

Distance:	9.5km (6m)
Maps:	OS 1:25,000 Pathfinder 1039, Golden Valley and 1016, Hay-on-Wye
Start Point:	Snodhill Castle, GR 321404
Public Transport:	Hereford to Brecon bus halts at nearby Dorstone
Refreshments:	None on route, pub in Dorstone

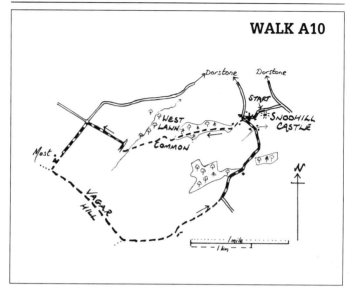

WALK A10

Sometimes the patchwork of woodlands and pastures, gates and stiles can seem a little restrictive. Then it is time to set off for the border hills, to stretch the legs with little need for careful routefinding. This is such a walk, from a ruined castle in a perfect situation, through woods and over commons to a breezy upland.

Snodhill Castle may have been at the back of the queue when evocative names were handed out, but it receives ample compensation in its positioning. Over the upper Golden Valley towards Moccas Park and Merbach Hill, until the eye focusses on wooded valleys nearer to hand, range the views. The castle was constructed in the late twelfth century, was strengthened in the early thirteenth century, but was ruinous by 1355. The border wars of the early fifteenth century gave it a further lease of life, but a bombardment by the Scots during the Civil War terminated its military career.

High on the mound are the remnants of the long, narrow, keep, with thick walls. It seems only to have comprised of a hall above a storage basement. Part of the curtain wall and a flanking tower also remain.

*View from
Snodhill Castle*

Descend to the road and go left to a crossroads, where cross over (No Through Road). The road climbs between tall oaks and larch, with a hazel understorey. Carry straight along a track at the point where the road bends sharply left, uphill - ignore a track going down to the right. Continue to the gate to West Lawn Common.

Initially keep left, but at a fork go right, contouring along the hillside. This path eventually meets the stream at a gate. Cross the stream and climb to the road, where go right. The road bends left and heads ruler-straight to a crossroads. All roads to this point are drawn with the same geometric precision - we go left.

The road climbs past the communications tower, and then the mass of the Black Hill and Hay Bluff loom into sight ahead. At the gate go left. You are now on the crest of Vagar Hill, able to let your vision roam to distant horizons (except for the wet patches). When the skylarks are in full song this is definitely the right place to be.

At the end of the ridge bear left, through a gate of sorts. At the next gate take the opportunity to switch to the opposite side of the hedge. When a sunken lane appears on the right, move into it, and proceed to the road, where go left. Soon the road falls steeply to Snodhill, with the castle back in view.

WALK A11:
Weobley

Distance:	7km (4¹/₂m)
Map:	OS 1:25,000 Pathfinder 994, Leominster and 993, Kington
Start Point:	Bell Square, Weobley, GR 402515
Public Transport:	Hereford to Kington and some Hereford to Tillington bus services
Refreshments:	Pubs and cafes in Weobley
Other Information:	*A Guide to the Village of Weobley*, (small charge)

Here in the heartland of half-timbered Herefordshire it is difficult to choose the village which has the finest selection of these magpie buildings, let alone which is the prettiest. Certainly Weobley must be one of the front runners, a former market town which fell on hard times and so escaped the worst deprivations of the "improvers". This walk also visits some of the adjoining countryside, including pleasant parkland and an outstanding house.

Bell Square has fourteenth-century houses to the south. Walk towards the village centre and turn up Church Road. The soaring spire of the church is the second highest in the county, a reminder of wealthy days. The tower is at such an angle to the main body of the church as to suggest that it was originally detached, and was later linked by the north aisle. Inside there are fifteenth-century alabaster effigies and a statue of Colonel John Birch, Civil War veteran and Member of Parliament. Be warned - it is said that if you

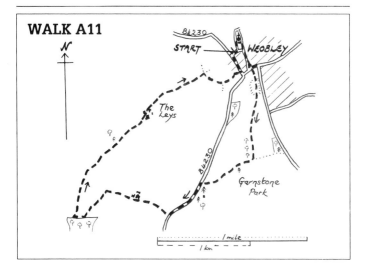

WALK A11

N

BL230
START
WEOBLEY
The Leys
BL230
Garnstone Park

1 mile
1 km

walk backwards seven times around each flight of steps to the churchyard cross you will see the Devil (the author felt unable to test this claim on your behalf).

From the church return to the village centre via The Pavement. The Red Lion Hotel occupies a prominent position on the corner of Broad Street, where we find a feast of half-timbered buildings, some dating back to the fifteenth century. Bear left where the street divides, on to Market Place. The rose garden marks the site of a much lamented market hall, demolished in 1840, a Mansion House in which thirty-three children were born to James Tomkins (by two wives), and other buildings destroyed by fire in 1943.

Briefly divert left on to High Street, with the seventeenth-century Unicorn on the left. On the corner with Hereford Road is The Throne, confusingly known as the Unicorn when King Charles I stayed here after the Battle of Naseby in 1645. Return to the village centre and turn left opposite the Market Place, towards the castle earthworks. Built shortly after the Conquest it saw action in the wars of Stephen and Matilda, being captured by King Stephen in 1138. Later it was a base for the powerful Walter de Braose. Now only the earthworks remain, an oval bailey surrounded by moats.

It is suspected that the eastern side survives to its original height.

From here pass through a gateway and bear slightly right, across parkland. Go through the next gate, but not the one after - instead turn right. You are in Garnstone Park, although the mansion of Garnstone Castle, built by Nash in 1807, was demolished in 1959.

Pass through two more gateways to the road, where go left for about 300m before turning right, down the track to Fenhampton. Now comes a frustrating detour to avoid a minor trespass. Do not pass through the gate at the end of the track, instead go through the one just before it on the left. Follow the field side, and then go right, along the outside of the wood. Turn right at the next field corner, and continue through another gate at the end of the field.

Cross the next field to a stile and footbridge, then keep the field side on your right - this is overgrown in high summer. Persevere to join a track to a farm. Keep left through the buildings (you may even see a waymark) to arrive in front of a truly outstanding house. The Leys displays natural exposed oak timbering, not the artificial black and white of so many half-timbered buildings. It must look much as it did when completed in 1589.

Take a stile on the left, just after the pond, follow the field side, and after another stile keep the edge of the field to your right. Aim for a stile at the top of a little rise. Now go right and then bear left to another stile on the opposite side of the field. One more stile to go, straight ahead, then along the field side to a yard, and so to the road. Go left, along Back Lane, passing the museum, to return to Bell Square.

WALK A12:
Monnington Walk

Distance:	6.5km (4m)
Map:	OS 1:25,000 Pathfinder 1016, Hay-on-Wye
Start Point:	Monnington Village, GR 372435
Public Transport:	Hereford-Rhyader and Hereford-Almeley bus service on main road
Refreshments:	None on route

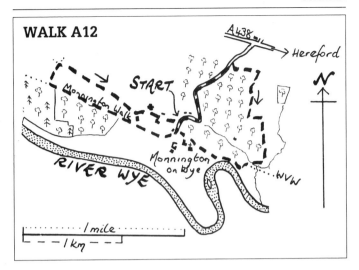

Monnington is no doubt grateful for being off the beaten track, away from the busy A438, and close by the River Wye. If apple orchards are much in evidence, then discovery that this is part of the Bulmer estates will not be a surprise. Visitors are made to feel welcome rather than an intrusion, and a further bonus is that this walk involves the minimum of ascent - ideal after Sunday lunch!

Start by the entrance to Monnington Court, a building largely of the seventeenth century, but with a fifteenth-century wing closest to the church. Turn your back on the Court to be confronted by Monnington Walk, an avenue of Scotch firs extending for fully 2.5km (1¹/₂m) to Brobury. The avenue was probably planted in 1628 to mark the election of William Tomkins as MP for nearby Weobley. The firs are interspersed with yews, and some replacement planting has taken place.

To the left may be seen some of the orchards, at their best in mid or late May when in full blossom. Woodland appears on the left - before being engulfed take a gate on the right and follow the field edge. At the next gate go right, along a track that can be very muddy in places. The track becomes metalled before rejoining the road at the telephone kiosk. Keep to the left and continue along the road.

The road is still surrounded by apple orchards. After the orchards on the right end by an oak tree you will find a stile in the hedge. Take this and follow the field margin as it goes left, then right. Officially the path goes through the copse on the right, but this is quite difficult, so go into the orchard on the right and keep to the edge to emerge in the field beyond the copse.

At the next angle in the field cross the border into the orchard and go left. The house in view ahead is Garnons - this house of 1860 replaced an Elizabethan mansion. The park was landscaped by Repton in 1791. Go right at the next corner, then right again, still on the perimeter of the orchards. Finally a ditch is approached - usually relatively dry, and bridged by a fallen tree. Once over you will find that you have joined the Wye Valley Walk. An informative sign states that 310 of Bulmer's 2,000 acres of apple orchards are to be found on the estate - a far cry from the cider firm's humble origins in Credenhill in 1887.

Continue ahead and go right, along the river bank at the point where it makes one of its great horseshoe loops with an island upstream. After leaving the river behind, Morgan horses may be seen in the fields on the left. The path then leads through the

Cider Mill at Monnington Court

churchyard. The church itself was rebuilt in 1679 for Uvedale Tomkyns, and many of the interior fitments are of that date. A path then leads back to the start point.

WALK A13:
Abbey Dore

Distance:	13km (8m)
Map:	OS 1:25,000 Pathfinder 1039 Golden Valley
Start Point:	Abbey Dore Church, GR 387303
Public Transport:	Hereford to Abbey Dore bus services
Refreshments:	Neville Arms, Abbey Dore; teas at Abbey Dore Court Gardens and Pen-twyn Cottage

The Golden Valley conjures up visions of the land of milk and honey - think of the difference it would have made if it was known as the Black Valley. In fact the Normans took the Welsh name for the little river that runs through the valley, "dwr" meaning black, and transformed it to their "d'or" meaning gold. This alchemy was not the only lasting change they made, for they also endowed the valley with an abbey, the remains of which are visited at the commencement of this walk. Thereafter this is a pleasant walk around a gentle area.

Walk down the path to the remains of Dore Abbey. Founded in 1147 by the Cistercian order, with their usual impeccable taste for remote yet scenic locations, the present building represents the western portion of the church built 1175-90. The tower was erected in the 1630s by Lord Scudamore, and many of the internal fitments also date from that time. Exceptions include two thirteenth-century effigies of knights.

Our route continues to the south of the church, via a kissing gate in a corner of the churchyard. Two more kissing gates follow, then over the field is a bridge spanning the River Dore. The path is now confined by a high fence until the road appears. Go left, and on the left is Abbey Court Gardens.

Enter the field opposite the gardens and follow the hedge - the

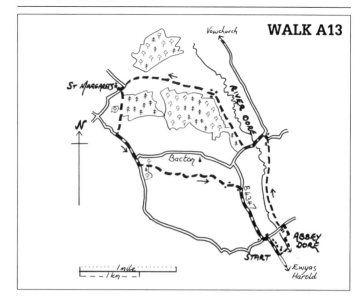

route is now waymarked. Go half right at a copse and over two stiles. The path leads to the rear of the hamlet of Riversdale, once a workhouse! At the road go left, then left again onto the B4347. Cross the river again, and at the woodland edge take a track to the right, leading to Newcourt Farm. On the right can still be discerned the route of the railway that ran to Hay-on-Wye until 1957. Pass through the farmyard, bearing left, in front of the farmhouse. Now comes one of those little quirks of our rights of way. A track leads up the hillside, but the right of way bears right, then climbs left by a hedge to rejoin the track.

For a short distance there are no stiles or other aids to navigation, so at the field corner steer between two distinct paths to cross a fence. Go right for about 200m, then half left, across another fence, and join a track just to the left of Tanhouse Wood.

Go left on the track to find the hamlet of St Margarets. The church lies slightly off our route, to the right. It possesses a few Norman fragments and a finely carved rood screen and loft dating from about 1520.

Back on the road, a track to the left leads towards Park and Maerdy Woods, but before being completely enfolded by the foliage a rickety stile on the right takes you into a field. Cross diagonally to another stile, and aim for the middle of the hedge ahead. After another stile keep to the field boundary.

At the next field bear right to the diagonally opposite corner, to emerge onto the road. Go left, continue past the junction with the Bacton road, and then go left again, through a gate just before a wood.

Enter the wood at a corner. The track leads to a gate - once through head diagonally downhill to a gate. Now follow the hedge of blackthorn and hawthorn to another gate and then a choice of no less than three more gates. Choose the one in the middle.

Cross the field diagonally (again!) to yet another gate, and follow the field boundary right. Pass through the next gateway and go left. Still more gateways ensue, and when the supply expires carry on to a vestigial hedge. Go right on a track which leads through an abandoned farmstead on its way to the road. Turn right for about 2km of not unpleasant road walking to return to the start.

WALK A14:

Skenfrith, Grosmont and Garway

Distance:	23km (14$^{1}/_{2}$m)
Map:	OS 1:25,000 Pathfinder 1064, Ross-on-Wye (West)
Start Point:	Skenfrith Castle GR 457202
Public Transport:	Some Hereford to Garway bus services also visit Skenfrith
Refreshments:	Pubs in Skenfrith & Grosmont, tea shop in Skenfrith
Other Information:	Cadw booklet *The Three Castles.* Leaflets at local churches

This is the longest walk in the book, along a part of the Monnow Valley steeped in history. The fortifications are a reminder that this has long been a border land, once fiercely fought over, if now tranquil and always pretty. Ancient castles, churches, dovecotes and bridges are locked into a landscape of hills, valleys, streams and rivers that are a microcosm of this romantic area.

The castle of Skenfrith provides a vivid reminder of those troubled years shortly after the Conquest, when Norman border lords sought to impose their rule on unwilling local inhabitants, and raiders from the fastnesses of the Welsh mountains. Although founded in the middle of the twelfth century most of the remains date from early thirteenth. The round tower is still impressive.

Upon leaving the castle go through a gate on the right to a

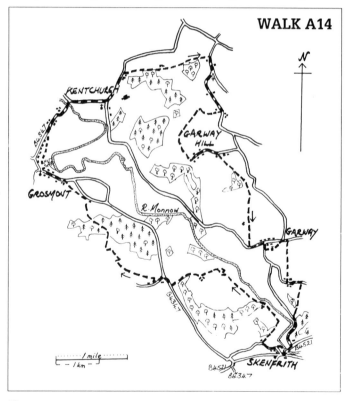

pasture overlooking the weir. The adjoining mill is one of the oldest in the area. Go left to the churchyard. The church itself is dedicated to St Bridget, and is contemporaneous with the castle. The furnishings are largely Jacobean, and at the end of the north aisle is an embroidered fifteenth-century cope - a treasure indeed. An extra curiosity is that the church tower once served as a dovecote.

Turn right, along the road. At Drybridge House cross the Norton Brook and go right, along a track which climbs twixt pretty banks, laden in springtime with primroses, wild strawberry flowers and violets. The track looks down on the Monnow before subsiding to Birch Hill. Just before the farm a stile on the right takes us to another stile at the side of the gate, and avoids the farmyard by another stile alongside a gate. A further stile, a ditch and then a stroll along the fieldside follow. Concentration can be transferred to the lovely surroundings as the path flirts with the river, passing through a sequence of gateways, then on to the farmstead of Trevonny.

Once through the farmyard join a track which leads by Box Farm, and its relics of agricultural machinery, to join a road. Turn right, then left at the next junction. Soon a yellow waymark points to the right, where the path zig zags uphill, enlivened in springtime by prolific clumps of daffodils. Things level out until at a new barn the track again zig zags to the right - still clearly waymarked. Go left at a fence, then right, over the crest of the ridge of Graig Syfyrddin, to enter woodland. Go left, then right through formerly coppiced trees.

On leaving the wood the path bears downhill over a sequence of waymarked stiles to join a green lane at the rear of a few houses at Little Cross. Go left and follow the fieldside downhill, veering left towards the bottom of the field to find a footbridge secreted in a gully. The route then continues downhill to a farm by the road.

Now cross the Tresenny Brook and head uphill towards Grosmont. Enter the churchyard by a gate on the left and wander around the outside. The church largely dates from 1180 to around 1300 and has an unusual dedication to St Nicolas of Myra. Enter the main doorway for a surprise. The main body of the nave is unrestored, a stark contrast to the many lovingly maintained interiors seen today. Interesting objects are scattered around - a crude stone effigy of a warrior, a solid oak hutch (or chest), church documents and much else.

Passing through the oak screen inserted by the Victorian restorer we can see that today's congregation is cosily housed in the crossing. The dog-tooth moulding around the thirteenth-century piscina in the chancel is particularly fine.

Leave the churchyard by the main gate and cross the road to enter the castle precincts. The name of the village derives from "gros mont" or big mound, and it is plain to see why. The castle was rebuilt by Hubert de Burgh in 1218 and is surrounded by a deep, if relatively dry, moat. The remains are still impressive, if dangerous to over-exuberant children.

Leaving by the south side, walk round to the north and along the field, until a gate onto the road appears on the left. Go right, down Cupid's Hill, to cross the Monnow. Supposedly Jack o'Kent from nearby Kentchurch Court struck a bargain for the Devil to construct a bridge here in exchange for the first soul to cross it. Upon completion Jack threw a bone over, so that a dog was the first to cross - this was in the days before the RSPCA.

Turn right at the junction, and shortly before Kentchurch Church go left on an unsigned road. On the right are the grounds of Kentchurch Court, rebuilt around 1800 by Nash and the home of the Scudamore family since at least the fourteenth century. One daughter married Owen Glendower, who was later outlawed by Henry Bolingbroke for supporting Richard II. He wandered the county in disguise and spent much time here. The panelled room in which he slept still survives.

At Bannut Tree Farm take a gateway set back to the left of the buildings and select a line across the hillside to a row of trees. This marks a path along a terrace, through a gate, over a stile and by the woodland edge. Soon begins the only unpleasant part of the walk - heavy Herefordshire mud (and worse!). Pass through two gates - at the second it is preferable to detour into the field. Things improve after the farmstead. Take the right hand of two gates facing you, then go over a stile on the left and head downhill.

Cross the stream above a confluence, then the second stream by a fallen tree acting as a bridge. After these Amazonian exploits climb uphill to a gate just to the left of the wood. Another two gateways follow, before bearing left to the road. Now go right. Keep

Skenfrith Castle

right at a fork by a chapel, now over-looking the amphi-theatre of the valley of the Garren Brook.

After about 1km take a lane to the right, detouring around the White House as Garway Hill is gained. Make for the brick structure which serves as the summit wind shelter. The views encompass the Monnow Valley, the Forest of Dean, and the Black Mountains. Leave by the broad track to the south-west, with an aerial view of Kentchurch Court to your right.

The grassy trod curves left to join a track, where bear left. Pass through a smattering of cottages, and then cross a fence stile adjoining a gate immediately after White Rocks Cottage. Walk down to a bridge over the stream and go right to cross a crude stile. Follow the field edge uphill, but towards the top cross diagonally to a small gate in the far corner. The field edge is now on your right.

On entering the next field cross diagonally to the right. Now follow the field edge to pass above The Lodge and join the farm track. Go left to join the road, where go left again and then right at the junction. Now turn along Church Way to the fascinating little church of Garway. The tower is at an angle to the nave and was originally detached. The church was granted to the Knights Templar in the late twelfth century, and the foundations of their earlier round building are exposed on the east side. Internally, the chancel arch is one of the finest features, with three rows of chevrons. There is also an old chest, carved from an oak tree trunk.

In the adjacent farmyard is a dovecote with 666 pigeonholes. A tablet has been deciphered as saying "istud columbarium factum fuit per Ricardum (1326)", although it is likely that Richard was repairing rather than building this structure.

Leave the churchyard by the gate at its highest point, follow the field edge, and at an angle head diagonally uphill to a gate in the far corner, opposite a cottage. Go right, and after a junction (yes, Bagwylldiart is in England) go through a gate set back on the right, just after a cottage. Follow the field margin to the right, pass through the left hand of a pair of gates, and look down on Garway as you march along.

The path becomes a track and goes through a farmyard. At the road go left. After about 400m take a stile on the right and head straight downhill. At the road go left, in the company of the Monnow again. Upon meeting the B4521 turn right to return to Skenfrith.

Primrose

WALK A15:
Penbridge and Eardisland

Distance:	8km (5m)
Maps:	OS 1:25,000 993, Kington and 994, Leominster
Start Point:	The Olde Steppes in Pembridge, GR 392582
Public Transport:	Pembridge is on the Leominster to Kington and Shobdon bus routes
Refreshments:	Ample selection in both villages, particularly Eardisland

Herefordshire is famed for its black and white villages of which Pembridge and Eardisland are amongst the finest. Linked by the River Arrow, on one side of which runs a public footpath and on the other a minor road, the walking forms a gentle interlude between two intriguing villages.

Stroll down the road in the direction of Leominster (right from the parking area). There are too many half-timbered buildings to describe, but each warrants individual attention, within an unplanned yet cohesive composition.

Turn left by the almshouses of 1686, noting the inscription, and upon entering a haulage yard take the gate to the left. At the other side of the field is a stile and a footbridge, then follow the field

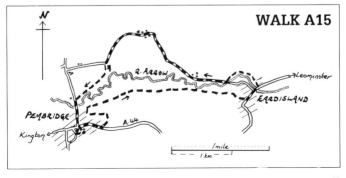

Bell tower, Penbridge

margin, which curves to the left. Pass through a gate of sorts to a green lane, then go over a stile on the right, along the rear of a few houses, to another stile. Now go right.

The path across these flat riverside meadows does not cling as closely to the Arrow as one may expect and desire. A series of stiles takes one across arable fields, at one point offering a tantalising glimpse of the river at a weir. Growing crops may force the field boundary to be followed into what appears to be a cul-de-sac, but then there is a stile hidden in the hedge on the right. Turn left and follow the field margin to another stile, after which you should head across the meadow to a road.

You are now in the village of Eardisland. Go left towards the bridge, which acts as a magnet for so many visitors. Here the Arrow is wide and tranquil with waterfowl dabbling about. Nearby is a cluster of fascinating buildings - just before the bridge is a seventeenth-century dovecote, capable of harbouring 800 birds, in the grounds of the largely timber-framed Mansion House. Over the bridge is the former grammar school, also timber-framed and boasting a whipping post. Slightly further along the Leominster

Wye Bridge, Hereford Cathedral behind

Giant's Cave and Herefordshire Beacon

Ross-on-Wye

Ferry across the Wye

road is the Staick House, which has a fourteenth-century central hall, still retaining its original sandstone tiles.

Walk upstream along the river on the Leominster side, and over a stile is a small mound, possibly a motte. Bear left through a caravan park, and keep to the left to find the road. Turn right along this minor road, which initially keeps close to the river. It then veers away to pass Broom before curving back. Take the track on the left, leading to the farmstead of Twyford. Cross the stile on the right and bear half left to a stile over the field. Another stile follows, and the next one is on to the road, where turn left.

The Arrow is crossed with inviting picnic spots beckoning. Walk up Bridge Street, at the top of which you are faced by the Olde Steppes, with its finely carved bargeboards, once a rectory and now a shop. Continue up the steps at the side of the shop to the church. Here is Pembridge's pride and joy, the detached bell tower which provides an abiding symbol of the village. It dates from the fourteenth century, and has a pyramidal roof housing the clock and bell mechanism. Much of the church is of similar date, as are some of the effigies, although many of the furnishings such as the pulpit, are Jacobean.

On leaving the church by the main door turn left to arrive at the market place. The sixteenth-century market house may have lost its upper storey, but still reminds us that this was once an important market town. It backs onto the New Inn - new as recently as 1311. Allegedly the treaty following the battle of Mortimers Cross was signed here. On returning to the main street go right to return to the start.

WALK A16:

Westhope Hill

Distance:	11km (7m)
Map:	OS 1:25,000 Pathfinder 994, Leominster
Start Point:	Queen's Wood Country Park Visitor Centre GR 506515
Public Transport:	On Hereford/Kidderminster/Birmingham bus route
Refreshments:	Cafe at the Visitor Centre
Further Information:	Free leaflet about the Country Park from the Information Centre

The Queen's Wood Country Park is not merely woodland with public access, but has an arboretum with interesting specimen trees and an exceptional viewpoint. What is more, it also serves as a good start point for walks along adjacent ridges. The walk out to Westhope Hill is simple, along one of these ridges. From the hill itself there are excellent views, and the return is along upland fields.

Queen's Wood was given to Herefordshire County Council in 1935, as a memorial of King George V's Silver Jubilee. The purchase was assisted by the Council for the Preservation of Rural England. The most visited part of what is now the Country Park is the Arboretum, which was created in 1945. The County Council has produced a free leaflet with a detailed plan of this part of the wood, and you are recommended to stray through, visiting the viewpoint and toposcope at your leisure.

Start from the Visitor Centre (once the Tannery in Leominster), and walk up the Lime Avenue to the rear. Curve to the left, join a track, and follow this out of the wood. Turn right and head downhill, then take the lane leading off to the left. Ignore a right fork, but at the next gateway leave the lane and head diagonally across the field to your right to a stile. Rejoin the lane, passing lonely Kipperknoll Cottage. Continue ahead at the point where the track curves downhill into woodland.

A sequence of waymarked gates and stiles now clearly delineates the route over and along the edges of the next five fields. The path then leads across a large field, arriving at a lane, alongside a pond. Go right to enter the scattered settlement of Westhope Hill. Turn right on reaching the metalled road, over the cattle grid onto the Common. Bear left (just to the right of the farms and cottages), then veer to the right to the top of the northern slope.

This is a place of popular resort, and no wonder, for the views are panoramic. Near at hand is Camp Wood, masking the ancient hill fort of Ivington Camp. Beyond is Leominster, then Titterstone Clee. Further to the left are the wooded hills around Croft Ambrey and the Mortimer Forest, looking over to the hinterland of mid-Wales.

From here pick up a track which takes you down into the far right-hand corner of the Common. Pass through a belt of trees and keep to the right of a farmstead to a gate on to a very minor road. Take the road straight ahead and bear right at the fork by Rose Cottage. At the end of the track go over a stile to the left of the gate and head for the gate facing you, in the shallow dry valley. Now

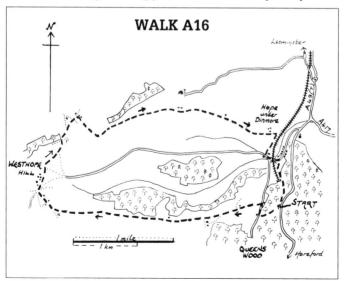

WALK A16

follow the field side, climb two more stiles and turn left.

Once over another stile bear slightly right to the next one, then straight ahead to a stile by a young oak tree. There are more stiles to come - the next is a little to the right, by three horse-chestnut trees. Now keep alongside the field boundary on the left until you spy a stile in the converging hedge, for which you should aim. Go straight over the field to a stile by the abandoned farmstead of Cold Ash. Keep along the tall hedge on the left, looking down from Winsley Hill to the head of a small valley.

Three more stiles now, and after a modern barn pick up a track which goes through a gate. Leave the track to cross to a stile half-hidden in the hedge to the left, just before the cattle grid. The path now falls rapidly towards the main Hereford to Shrewsbury railway line, but do not cross the line. Instead go right, and to the right of a cottage is a gate to the road. Turn left, pass under the railway, then go right, along a lane.

Leave the lane on the left, over a field, then into woodland. You will now understand that Dinmore means great hill, as you toil uphill. Cross one track and join another. Ignore crossing tracks as the drone of the A49 grows louder. Return to the Visitor Centre via the Memorial Stone.

WALK A17:
Bringsty common

Distance:	5.5 to 9.5km ($3^1/_2$ to 6m)
Map:	OS 1:25,000 Pathfinder 995, Bromyard
Start Point:	Bringsty Common - around GR 700550
Public Transport:	Bromyard and Hereford to Worcester bus services
Refreshments:	Live and Let Live pub on the Common
Other Information:	Lower Brockhampton open: end of March to end of September, Wednesday to Sunday (and Bank Holiday Mondays), 10.00am to 1.00pm and 2.00pm to 6.00pm (closes 4.00pm) October.

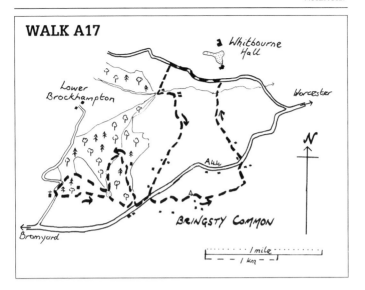

WALK A17

Bringsty Common is a rugged piece of upland which needs some exploration if its mysteries are to be uncovered. It has enough nooks and crannies to hide most of the Sunday afternoon trippers. This walk traverses the Common and some of the surrounding countryside, with the opportunity to add on one or more of the waymarked routes around the Brockhampton Estate.

At the eastern end of Bringsty Common is a telephone kiosk, opposite which a path leads off at the side of the former police house. Continue over the fields to the left of another house and then bear half right to a barely recognisable stile in the corner of the field. Once over it is best to detour to the left to avoid the worst of the soggy depression.

Back on your original line, go through a gate and bear right to another. Further along the side of the stream is a footbridge. Once over go through a gate on the right to rise to the road. From here Whitbourne Hall with its imposing portico can be seen. The design is based upon the Erechtheum in Athens. The hall was built in 1861/2 by Edward Bickerton Evans at a cost of £21,055, the result of a prosperous vinegar works in Worcester.

Walk to the left along the road for about 0.5km. A sign on the left points the way past The Old Mill, down in Paradise Dingle. Please close the gates behind you. Bear left to Home House Farm, then right, through the farm yard, and so into the orchards. Go through the left-hand of a pair of gates and along the field side. Pass through a gateway, along the field edge, and over a stile. Pass between two cottages and bear right at a fork.

You are now on Bringsty Common, dotted with cottages and criss-crossed by tracks. Keep left at the next fork, over a track, and then bear right. Keep right and cross the next track to arrive in front of a cottage, and walk up the bank to the road. If the confusion of tracks causes problems just head towards the sound of traffic.

Now a decision must be made. If you wish to visit the National Trust's Brockhampton estate (recommended) go right, along the road. Just prior to the start of the high estate wall a track to the right leads to a gate piercing the wall. Once through, an information board shows three waymarked routes, which may be varied - the blue and red ones take you through the woods to the right, and should initially be followed. The blue route is slightly longer than the red one, but both bring you to the Lawn Pool dam. Here cross over, now on the yellow route, and a rising terrace path leads into the woods around Brockhampton House. There is a side view of the mid-eighteenth-century red brick building, and a retrospect of Ankerdine Hill. The House is let on a long lease to an insurance company, so there is no public access to it or the immediate grounds.

Pass through the belt of woodland to arrive at a tarmac track. Lower Brockhampton is about 1.25km to the right, but even if you decide to make a separate visit there, it should not be missed. Built around 1400, and still guarded on three sides by a moat, this half-timbered masterpiece forms a charming and picturesque grouping completed by a tiny detached gatehouse. The bargeboards facing the world date from the 1952 National Trust restoration, those on the inner side being the original fifteenth-century article. The panels were originally filled with a mixture of resin, beeswax and sawdust. Nearby are the ruins of a Norman chapel.

If this detour is rejected for the present, go left along the driveway on leaving the wood. Just before the second cattle grid and on the right is the "new" chapel of 1798. Our route bears left over the grid, still following the yellow waymarks, along the side of the park amidst horse-chestnuts and cedars to a stile. Cross another drive and head down the hill, now with oaks and walnuts present. To the right of the Pool is a stile by a gate. Bear left towards the wood, then climb the hill alongside the wood and at the wall go left, back into the woods. A little along this path is the hole in the wall to return to the Common.

Go left and cross the main road on to a track leading to the main part of the Common. Now climb towards the clump of horse-chestnuts shielding the triangulation column. This is a pleasant spot to relax and survey the surrounding rolling countryside. Descend in the opposite direction from your ascent, and now you are on your own. The Common sports a myriad of tracks and paths traversing its knobbly terrain. Part of the fun is in a leisurely exploration, discovering the Live and Let Live pub and an unlikely football pitch.

Do not venture too far south (right), and from the vicinity of the football pitch gradually return to the road (which is usually within earshot), to find the start point.

WALK A18:
By River Teme and Sapey Brook

Distance:	15.5km (9¹/₂m)
Maps:	OS 1:25,000 Pathfinder 995, Bromyard and 973, Great Witley
Start Point:	Whitbourne Church GR 725569
Public Transport:	Hereford to Worcester bus service 1km S of start, or Worcester/Tenbury service to Clifton-on-Teme
Refreshments:	The Lion in Clifton-on-Teme, the Live and Let Live in Meadow Green

Even in a land of such beautiful rivers as Britain, the Teme must rank as one of the loveliest. Little known it may be, but its tributary, the

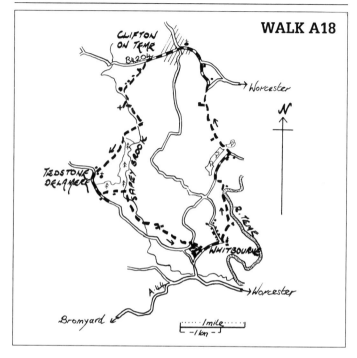

Sapey Brook, is positively secretive, and yet possesses an intimate charm that can only be explored on foot. This is an opportunity to glimpse both these valleys at their best, and ample time should be allowed to linger amidst sylvan and pastoral beauty spots little suspected outside the immediate locality.

Whitbourne Church is an amalgam of styles, ranging from the Norman font and south nave doorway, through the thirteenth-century chancel and south nave wall, to the fourteenth-century tower and the nineteenth-century aisle. It is built over a running spring, which may have been used for baptisms, and on the north wall is a fifteenth-century cope.

Two bishops are buried here, for next door Whitbourne Court was once the summer palace of the Bishops of Hereford. It was extended by Colonel Birch in the seventeenth century and again in the last century. Across the road the Venetian windows of the rectory are mirrored in the gates.

Now set off along the lane that leads north of the church, leading past the imposing sewage works near which the Boat Inn once stood at a ferry crossing. Enter the riverside pastures, with a tree-clad bank on one side and the alder-lined river on the other. When in flood the river may be a metre or more deep above this footpath.

One must soon turn aside and clamber up the bank at Scar Coppice. On leaving the wood continue ahead, over a field to a gateway, where turn right. The road passes Lower Tedney Farm, but at a sharp right-hand bend enter the field on the left. Climb up the hill, initially following the field margin. Veer to the right to enter the wood at an angle, although it is first worth pausing to look back down the Teme Valley. The track leads up through the wood, turning right at the margin to leave it. Now follow the field edge to Ayngstree Farmhouse.

Pass through the garden to join a concrete road at the rear of the house. Stride along to Woodmanton Farm. As the rights of way across the fields to Clifton are blocked, the farm road must be followed to the main road, where turn left. Take care, especially where the verge is narrow, but soon a footpath commences, leading to the village of Clifton on Teme.

Clifton is a pretty little village, especially in summer when the streets are ablaze with flowers in tubs, hanging baskets, and anywhere else they will grow. The church of St Kenelm has a thirteenth-century nave, chancel and tower, but was rebuilt in the nineteenth century. It contains an effigy of a cross-legged knight and tablets by the wood-carver Grinling Gibbons.

Leave the village by the Harpton road, and turn left along the No Through Road to Sapey Old Church. The road drops into the enchanted valley of the Sapey Brook, to cross the brook itself in an impressive little gorge. It is worth continuing to the abandoned Norman church, even if it does mean some retracing of steps. Services are held here now and then; at harvest time the straw pews and corn dollies give it an atmospheric character, harking back to primitive days.

Return down the road, and at a lay-by some steps lead down to the brook. A footbridge stands at the entrance to fairyland, the brook gouging down into the soft rocks, side streams splashing down, all overhung by trees with the light glancing through. Too soon the path climbs away, up past Waste Cottage and then high above the valley.

The path curves into a side valley, a place to linger rather than pause. A small stream tumbles over a waterfall, depositing tufa as it does. Tufa is calcium carbonate which has been dissolved in the water and is released when the pressure is reduced. A few metres upstream a miniature waterfall feeds a little pool, the sort most gardeners would be delighted to have as a feature in their gardens. Drag yourself away and at a gate bear left along a recent path diversion which by-passes Tidbatch. The clothing of conifers disguises the steepness of the valley side. When the path curves into another tributary valley pass through a gate on the right immediately after a solitary cottage to drop quickly to the valley floor.

A modern footbridge crosses the brook - sadly there are no riverside rights of way here. Climb past derelict Line House Farm into Tedstone Delamere, where go left. Just down the road, on the left, is the little church of St James which stands in splendid isolation amidst parkland, looking pensively over the Sapey Valley, perhaps remembering the village that also once stood here. Although heavily restored by Sir Gilbert Scott in the last century some interesting details remain. Two Norman windows and quoins at the west end are of tufa (as seen earlier in situ). There is a late medieval screen, an old hourglass in the porch, and a rather special fourteenth-century churchyard cross.

Now continue down the road and turn left along the track to Pixhill. Pass in front of the house and go downhill, crossing a forestry track. A footbridge to the right will take you over the Sapey Brook, then walk through the pastures to the right to another footbridge, recrossing the brook. Continue ahead, over a hump-backed bridge with a weir below. Ahead, and to the left, a gate takes the path uphill, past an extensive rabbit warren. The next stile requires care.

Go left upon reaching a lane and when level with the last farm building pass through a gate on the right. Through another gate, across the farmyard, then bear left and follow the fieldside. When faced by two gates take the one on the left, and continue ahead by the hedge. A stile and then a kissing gate lead to a road, where go right, then left. Bear left again by the school to return to Whitbourne.

WALK A19:
Ledbury and Wellington Heath

Distance:	8km (5m)
Maps:	OS 1:25,000 Pathfinder 1041, Ledbury and Much Marcle, 1018, Great Malvern
Start Point:	The Market House, Ledbury, GR 711377
Public Transport:	By rail from Paddington or Birmingham on the Hereford/Abergavenny line; by bus from Hereford or Great Malvern
Refreshments:	A wide variety of pubs, cafes and restaurants in Ledbury; The Farmers Arms in Wellington Heath
Other Information:	*The Footpaths of Ledbury* , *Ledbury Walkabout* (small charge)

Ledbury has been the subject of enthusiastic comment by many visitors over the years. A historic market town, it has an Elizabethan core with some marvellous buildings. What is more, it is only a short walk from beautiful countryside, particularly in to the crumpled limestone ridges and valleys to the north. That is where this walk leads, to find Wellington Heath clinging to either side of a small valley, before returning through orchards and woods.

Ledbury Market House is one of the most impressive examples of the genre. Surmounting sturdy chestnut pillars, it was built during the mid seventeenth century, and is attributed to John Abel, the king's carpenter. From here stroll up narrow, cobbled Church Lane, a scene which has graced many calendars, as half-timbered houses crowd in on a view drawn by the church spire ahead.

First on the left are the Town Council offices, now open on certain days so that the ancient wall paintings discovered during a

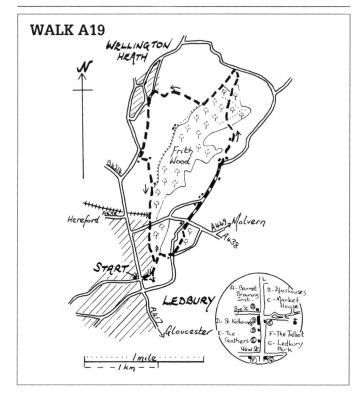

WALK A19

recent restoration can be inspected. A little higher up on the right is the folk museum, and the last building on the left is the Old Grammar School, dating from 1480 to 1520. The ground floor is now a Heritage Centre.

Continue past the seventeenth-century Church House and Abbot's Lodge in to the churchyard. The church is almost of cathedral proportions, with some Norman remains such as the main doorway with its chevron surround. Much of the exterior dates from around 1280 to 1340. It has a detached tower, the lowest part being of the thirteenth century, surmounted by a 38m spire. Inside are some interesting effigies, brasses and slabs including a thirteenth-century effigy of a priest. Every third hour the bells play a well-known hymn tune.

Proceed down the pathway flanked by high walls almost opposite the main porch. At the road turn right. At a sharp left-hand bend continue ahead up the path in to Dog Hill Wood, criss-crossed by paths. When faced by a bench take a right turn, and just as the path levels out look for a signpost set back on the right. This points downhill, across a field, with views over to Herefordshire Beacon.

Pass through a kissing gate and by a pond to a minor road - straight across another path enters a wood and climbs once more. It then drops in to a gully and turns left. To the right is Upper Hall Quarry, a Site of Special Scientific Interest (on private property) on account of the geological exposure of the Wenlock Limestone overlain by shales of the Lower Ludlow formation. On the main path, take the staircase to the right and then turn right, through a gate and over a field.

Emerge at the crossroads and continue along the Coddington road ahead. At Upper Mitchell Farm go through the farmyard, with disused hop kilns to the left, and climb the track past an isolated cottage. Bear left immediately before the next gate to enter Frith Wood, but first turning to admire the prospect of the Malvern Hills, with Herefordshire Beacon and the Eastnor Park obelisk prominent.

Cross a forestry track and take a path which eventually recrosses the track. Over a stile the path is surrounded by giant burdock and brambles, which contrive to grab your attention. No wonder Herefordshire brambles are nick-named "lawyers".

Leave the wood and downhill to the left is a stile. Once over, go through the gate on the

Jenny Wren on brambles

left, along a lane. Leave this by bearing right just as the wood is re-entered. The path now runs along the woodland margin. You could continue on this path to Ledbury, but the diversion to Wellington Heath is recommended, so take a stile on the right. Cross a footbridge in the valley bottom and go left. On leaving the fenced path go half right to a gate and stile. Why is the stile constructed like this?

At the road go left, passing the Farmers Arms. The village stands on the slopes of a steep-sided valley, and has declared itself to be the independent republic of Monkey Island. The navvies who constructed the railway through Ledbury were billeted here, and were known as "monkies".

Go left at the next sharp right-hand bend, over a stile, and head for the gate in the bottom left-hand corner of the field. Now follow more of those odd stiles - by now you should have guessed why they have that sliding flap, particularly if you have a dog with you! Cross a footbridge and climb to the right, through orchards. Once upon a time hop-pickers descended on this area, nowadays fruit pickers bring tents, caravans and barbecues.

At Frith Cottages go left, towards Briars Hundred, in the centre of the orchard, where go right. Through the plum trees, then the garden of Little Frith, on footpath LR15. Follow the field boundary to a gate, join a track and go right. Cross the road to re-enter Dog Hill Wood, and take the path along its fringe, with glimpses over the rooftops of Ledbury, to rejoin your outward route.

WALK A20:
Hereford City

Distance:	6km (4m)
Map:	None required
Start Point:	Wye Street car park (by the old bridge), Hereford, GR 509295
Public Transport:	Rail from Shrewsbury, Worcester and Abergavenny; Bus services to Cardiff, Abergavenny, Brecon & Rhyader,

Leominster, Ledbury etc.
Refreshments: Take your pick.

Hereford is quite cosy as cities go. Small, compact even, with its remaining historic core close by the banks of the River Wye. It is but a brief walk to riverside meadows. Other interesting features range from the ancient cathedral and city walls, through industrial relics, to the bustling shopping centre of today.

From the car park walk briefly towards the playing fields, then left to the riverside path, and left again to the Wye Bridge, of the late fifteenth century. "Hereford" is derived from "Army Ford", the ford in question (by the bridge) dating back at least as far as Roman

WALK A20: HEREFORD CITY

1. Waterworks Museum
2. Museum of Cider
3. The Bulmer Railway Centre
4. City Museum & Art Gallery

5. St John Medieval Museum
6. The Old House
7. Cathedral
8. Castle Green

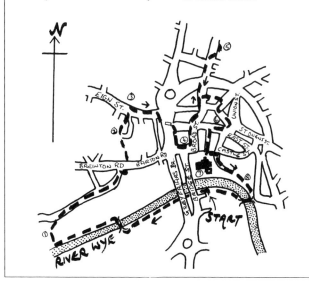

times. Cross the road and descend the steps, again along the river bank. Look back towards the Wye Bridge, with the Cathedral looming behind. One arch of the bridge differs from the others, having to be rebuilt following destruction during the Civil War.

Pass under the new road bridge, with playing fields already appearing. Walk up the steps of the old railway bridge and cross the river. The former rail line is now a valuable cycleway into the city centre. Go down the steps on the left over the bridge and continue along the riverbank. A track to the right leads towards the Herefordshire Waterworks Museum, its chimney overtopped by the watertower on the hill behind. The Museum has a number of working engines, but has limited opening hours on some Sundays and Bank Holiday afternoons during the summer.

Continue up the slope to the road, where go right. Just before joining Barton Road go down a path on the right to the cycleway and pass under the road. Keep to the path on the left around the perimeter of the supermarket car park. Standing back on the left at the top of the car park is the Cider Museum. The full story of cider, from apple orchard, through harvest, milling and pressing, to the final product is told here in attractive displays. The Museum opens from April to October, 7 days per week, 10.00am to 5.00pm, and from November to March, Monday to Saturday, 1.00pm to 5.00pm.

Proceed to cross busy Eign Street. At the side of Bulmer's modern offices is the entrance to the Bulmer Railway Centre. Two working locomotives, King Edward V and Princess Elizabeth, are usually to be found here, along with many other exhibits. The centre opens from Easter/April to September inclusive, weekends and Bank Holidays only, 2.00pm to 5.00pm. There are also steam open days and steam operated brake van rides on some Sundays and Bank Holidays - check with the Tourist Information Centre.

From the Railway Centre turn towards the city centre and recross Eign Street. At the junction go briefly right onto Greyfriars and down the subway on the right. Once on the opposite side of the ring road go right. The remains of the city walls are at your side, this length terminated by the only two surviving semi-circular towers. Towards the end you will see a cannonball cemented into the wall. Turn into St Nicholas Street, with a plaque marking the site of the former Friar's Gate. Continue ahead, with the bulky mass of the

Cathedral as impressive ahead as it has been for many centuries.

Along King Street, and left onto Broad Street, passing the Library, Museum and Art Gallery. Broad Street is terminated by All Saints Church, dating from about 1290, with a chained library and fourteenth-century misericords, as well as a good example of a wall painting on the east wall. Most people will remember this church by its twisted spire, now straightened.

Go right and then left onto Widemarsh Street. Walk along here and across the ring road, in due course to find on the right the St John Medieval Museum. Whilst the Museum is dedicated to the Ancient Order of St John, especially the days of the Crusades, there are other curiosities. These include a skeleton (thought to be of a fifteenth-century Abbot, but looking much like any other skeleton), and representations of Nell Gwynne, Charles II favourite, who was a native of this city. Opening hours are 2.00pm to 5.00pm daily (except Mondays and Fridays) from Easter to September.

Retrace your steps, again over the ring road. Turn left, towards the new shopping centre of Maylord Orchards, then right to High Town, where the Old House stands proudly. This is the sole survivor of what must have been an impressive range of half-timbered buildings known as Butcher's Row. Built in 1621, it has been furnished and equipped internally to be in keeping with that century.

Go right, along the pedestrianised area. Almost opposite the façade of the Market Hall is the narrow passage of Capuchin Lane. Take care crossing East Street to pedestrianised Church Street. A plaque indicates where Roger Kemble, founder of the great acting dynasty which included Sarah Siddons, was born in 1721 (between Nos.28 and 29). At No.20 lived the cathedral organist, Dr Sinclair, who was frequently visited by Edward Elgar. There are also many fascinating shops - don't miss the offshoot of Capuchin Yard.

Now, at last, it is time to pay homage to the Cathedral Church of St Mary the Virgin and St Ethelbert the King. The See was founded in 676, and there was a stone building here before the Conquest. The present building dates from around 1080 and is a blend of styles from Norman through Early English and Decorated to Perpendicular. A trip up the tower is an unforgettable experience, but the contents of the Cathedral are more interesting than the structure itself. The Chained Library is the largest in the world, and the Muniment Room contains 30,000 documents from Anglo-Saxon times onwards. The undoubted treasure is the Mappa Mundi, a thirteenth-century map of the world which is a work of both scholarship and antiquity.

Emerging from the north porch, go right to Castle Street, then turn right down Quay Street. This leads to Castle Green, where a succession of castles have stood since at least 1050, none of which seem to have had a long life. It was subject to siege in 1138 and 1140, during the wars of Stephen and Matilda. It also stood as a defence against Welsh raids. One lighter story surrounds the imprisonment of Henry III and Prince Edward in 1265. Edward organised horse races whilst allowed to exercise outside the castle walls. Having tired his guard's horses he then escaped on his own! On the northern side the castle pool is a fragment of the former moat. A monument to Admiral Lord Nelson (a frequent visitor to the city) stands on the Green.

Continue down the steps to a path, and turn right over the Victorian suspension bridge. Take the path half right. On the right is an embankment, part of the Rowe ditch earthworks which defended this part of the city south of the river, and hence the bridgehead. Shortly you will arrive back at the start point.

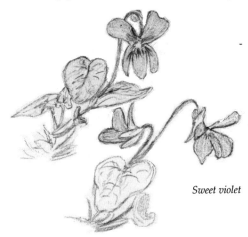

Sweet violet

MALVERN HILLS

INTRODUCTION

The Malvern Hills rear up from the Severn Plain like a recumbent dinosaur. Seen from the M5 their undulating silhouette often appears grey, yet at closer quarters the steep slopes are seen to be cloaked in a dazzling variety of greens and browns, a smattering of multi-hued buildings and a lattice of paths and tracks. Whilst not overly high the contrast with the low-lying Midlands plain renders them impressive as one draws nearer. Who can improve upon Celia Fiennes' description of the hills as "of at least 2 or 3 miles up and are in a Pirramidy fashion on the top".

The Hills are often quite steep, yet they are crossed at key points by motor roads, and the paths are so comprehensive that easily-graded and well-surfaced routes can be found to the highest points - and what views are then conveyed! Panoramic, aerial even, revealing the contrast between the sedate Worcestershire countryside to the east and the more undulating and heavily wooded terrain of Herefordshire to the west. The horizon is completed by the Black Mountains of Wales, the Shropshire Hills, the Cotswolds and the Forest of Dean.

The Hills are girdled by attractive communities, most notable of which is Great Malvern - almost the archetypal English spa town. The pride of the town is its Priory church, but it is also blessed with a wealth of Georgian and more especially Victorian buildings. It has its own share of history - the growth of the spa and the water cure is a story in itself, but the literary and musical connections are unparalleled for such a small community - Langland, Elgar, Jenny Lind, George Bernard Shaw, to name but a few. Today it maintains a cultured air in the shadow of the primeval hills.

Geology and Landscape

If the rolling acres (or hectares) of Herefordshire have a comparatively simple geological history, the 16km (10 miles) range of the Malvern Hills represent a geological conundrum. Here are much altered Precambrian rocks, suspected to be the oldest in England. The interpretation of these rocks remain a matter for academic debate, hence what follows is a highly simplified description.

To the east the relatively flat low-lying lands are underlain by Triassic rocks, deposited in desert conditions around 250 million years ago and up to 1,520m (5,000ft) in thickness. By contrast the oldest of the Malvernian rocks are metamorphic - they crystallised from sediments under extreme pressure 580 to 600 million years ago. The original rocks may have been shales or sandstones which originally formed about 1,000 million years ago.

These metamorphic rocks represent only 5% of the total, and include schist, gneiss, quartzite, marble and amphibolite. 75% are plutonic igneous rocks, mainly of a coarse-grained nature. This suggests that they were formed as a result of an oceanic plate being subsumed at an island arc or continental margin. This process continues elsewhere in the world today - for example the Pacific plate is disappearing beneath South America, giving rise to the Andes and their volcanic and other igneous phenomena. The remaining 20% are younger igneous rocks, especially dolerite.

Anyone walking the hills will notice that they do not form a simple north-south line. Herefordshire Beacon has been pushed westwards, so that the southern part of the chain is slightly dislocated from the northern part. In fact the Malvernian rocks are both broader and higher to the north than to the south - landscape here is quite a good guide to the underlying rocks. Chase End Hill has also been displaced.

To the east of Herefordshire Beacon are Broad Down and Tinkers Hill. These are composed of ancient volcanic rhyolite and spilites that are younger than the Malvernian rocks. In other words, whilst the main mass was intruded underground, these conform more closely to the popular idea of volcanic activity.

To the west of the Malverns are younger rocks. First are those of Cambrian age (600-500 million years ago) - largely the Hollybush Sandstone, and the Whiteleaved Oak or Black Shales, and the Bronsil or Grey Shales. These are found immediately to the west of Midsummer, Ragged Stone and Chase End Hills. They are believed to have formed in a shallow sea basin. The shales form areas of more subdued relief, but there are wooded knolls on the harder dolerite of a dyke swarm.

THE MALVERN HILLS
Simplified Geology

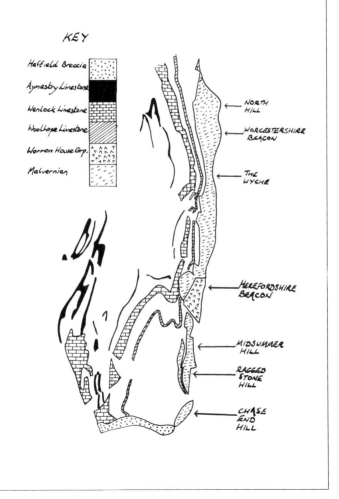

KEY

Hatfield Breccia
Aymestry Limestone
Wenlock Limestone
Woolhope Limestone
Warren House Grp.
Malvernian

NORTH HILL

WORCESTERSHIRE BEACON

THE WYCHE

HEREFORDSHIRE BEACON

MIDSUMMER HILL

RAGGED STONE HILL

CHASE END HILL

85

The Silurian (435-395 million years ago) forms a more varied landscape to the west of the Hills. This is due to the alternating nature of limestones and more easily eroded shales which give rise to ridges and valleys. In the northern part of the range the limestone ridges run close to and parallel to the Malverns themselves, but to the south they run further away. There are siltstones and mudstones amongst the limestones.

Wenlock Limestone is widely displayed. This is a grey limestone interspersed with layers of calcareous shales and mudstones. The Ridgeway, which arcs from below Herefordshire Beacon to Eastnor Park, is a good example of an outcrop of this limestone, typically clothed with trees. The younger Aymestry Limestone is responsible for the complex series of ridges (such as Oyster Hill) to the north of Ledbury.

All of these rocks resulted from a transgression of the sea over the eroded Cambrian or Precambrian landscape. They were laid down in shallow seas, and many of them - especially the shales - are rich in fossils such as brachiopods, trilobites and lamellibranches. Later came the Old Red Sandstone, described in the Herefordshire section.

The simplified geological map does not show the many faults or folds that also determine the landscape of this characterful area.

Natural History

The upper part of the Hills may seem to be relatively bare grassland. The common grasses such as sheep's fescue and common bent predominate on the acidic areas, although here and there you may also see harebells. Where the underlying rocks are base-rich the vegetation may include crested hair-grass and wild thyme. Flushes on Swinyard Hill host jointed rush, lousewort, common spike-rush and marsh pennywort. Lower down the hillside swathes of bracken are interspersed with bluebells and wood anemones.

Also lower down are varied woodlands - in drier areas sessile oak, birch and hazel, but ash and wych elm in the flushed areas. Plants include wood sorrel, yellow archangel and ramsons. You might also find climbing corydalis and violet helleborine.

Wildlife includes butterflies such as the high brown, dark green and pearl bordered fritillaries, the wood white, and, on open grassland, the grayling. Also on open ground skylarks, meadow pipits and wheatears are seen, in an area in which birdlife is prolific. Wood warblers, willow warblers, pied flycatchers, hawfinches and whitethroats occur in woodland. In autumn migrating ring ouzels and, later, snow buntings pass through. There is a large winter colony of lesser horseshoe bats. Polecats may possibly also be seen.

To the east of the central Hills is Castlemorton Common, an area of rough grassland, marsh and scrub. On the weakly acid areas are sorrel and tormentil, whereas in base-rich zones stemless thistle and mouse-ear hawkweed occur. In drier parts green woodpeckers visit the hummocks of anthills, often adorned by wild thyme.

Scrub includes the western and common gorse, hawthorn, blackberry and dog rose. Unusual is the quantity of pollarded black poplars - some eighty in total. Birds include the great grey shrike, snipe, reed bunting, whitethroat, yellowhammer and dunnock. Those with acute hearing may discern the call of the grasshopper warbler.

Prehistory and History

The prehistory of the Malvern area is closely linked with that of Herefordshire, described earlier. There are two fine hillforts on the southern part of the Hills. On Herefordshire Beacon is British Camp, one of the most distinctive profiles in the district. 2km (1$^1/_4$m) of earthworks encompass 13 hectares (32 acres) which could have accommodated up to 2,000 people. Further south is the Midsummer Hill/Hollybush Hill complex. Founded about 470BC it could also have held up to 2,000 people.

The area then retreated into the mists of history, with no mention of Roman intervention (if one discounts the legend of Caratacus' last stand being on Herefordshire Beacon) nor of Dark Age battles.

Norman times saw the creation of the Royal Forest of Malvern, governed on behalf of the King by the Lord of Hanley Castle. The Priory church was founded in 1085. The Forest became a Chase when it passed from royal hands into those of Gilbert de Clare, Earl of Gloucester. It was he (the Red Earl) who constructed the ditch along the crest of the Hills, to prevent his deer from escaping to the lands of the Bishop of Hereford to the west.

Piers Plowman was born during the fourteenth century, the

creation of William Langland, possibly a resident of Colwall parish. Langland later lived in London. His satire on the contrast between rich and poor contains the line "In a May morning on Malvern Hills".

The church was largely rebuilt in the Perpendicular style during the fifteenth century, but the Norman columns remain, also the west window reputedly gifted by Richard III. This was once a scene of the Last Judgement, but now contains fragments from other windows. The tiny township bought the church for its own use at the Dissolution of the monasteries. Although £20 may seem a small price to have paid one must remember that even 250 years later Malvern could only boast 800 inhabitants. The church remains one of the glories of the town, externally of multi-hued Cradley stone, internally with medieval stained glass considered second only to that of York Minster. There are more than 1,000 locally made encaustic tiles and fine carved misericords. It is visited on Walk B1.

As late as 1830 there were only about fifty houses in Malvern itself. Then came the water cure. The springs on the Hills had been widely known since Elizabethan times, and in the eighteenth-century publication of John Wall's analysis of the purity of the water and its alleged curative properties gave rise to some popularity.

Initially the Wells area to the south of Great Malvern was the centre of this modest industry. The opening of the Library and Baths (Walk B1) in 1819-23 caused an irrevocable shift to what is now the town centre. The central block of the Foley Arms Hotel dates from 1810, and the Belle Vue Hotel from 1816/17. Paths and shelters were built on the Hills, and donkeys were employed for transport from 1817. The Duchess of Kent and Princess Victoria visited in 1831.

By 1841 the population had grown to 2,768, yet with poor roads and a poverty stricken populace the town was a far cry from what it was soon to become.

In 1842 James Wilson arrived in Malvern. He was a student of Vincenz Priessnitz, the Czechoslovakian exponent of hydropathic remedies. James Gully, another believer in natural cures also arrived and the two set about building and converting properties for their patients. Gladstone, Dickens, Tennyson, Darwin and Florence Nightingale were amongst the more famous visitors.

The cure itself verged on the sadistic. Woken at 5.00am, patients were wrapped in cold, wet sheets and blankets, then sat in a cold bath. A walk to a spring came before breakfast. Other delights included the cold douche, a hogshead (240 litres) of cold water poured from a height of 6m on to the victim for up to $1^1/2$ minutes.

The opening of the railway (to Malvern Link by 1859) and the turnpiking of the roads by 1860 at long last resulted in decent communications. By 1868 forty-four trains per day ran through Malvern - even today it retains an Inter-City service.

This was the zenith of the cure's popularity. By the 1860s it was in decline, and it had vanished by 1891. Yet a lasting legacy remained. Land in Great Malvern was released by the major landowners for development from the mid-nineteenth century. Strict and detailed controls were imposed by the vendors, such as minimum plot size and that no two properties were to be alike. The reputation of the town enabled it to attract public and private schools, the most notable being Malvern College which opened in 1865. From an initial twenty-four pupils it had grown to a total of 600 boys by the turn of the century.

The modern town rests upon a varied mixture of employment. From the Second World War radar and telecommunications research and development has become a major employer. Schools, tourism and smaller industries, such as the hand-crafting of Morgan cars, are others. Indeed, the Santler, reputedly the first motor car ever made in Britain, was built at Malvern Link.

The town of Great Malvern retains much of its Victorian style and atmosphere. The hills and commons owe their present state of care to the Malvern Hills Conservators, founded by an Act of 1884. Their early history was one of successes mixed with frustrations. Probably their greatest victory was in gradually eliminating quarrying from the Hills - George Bernard Shaw wrote to *The Times* in 1929 that the industry was changing the Malvern Hills into the Malvern Flats. The last quarry was closed in 1977. Nowadays the major threats are over-use by pedestrians, mountain bikers, hang-gliders and the like, with the frequent ravages of fire.

Musical and Literary Connections

A veritable catalogue of notable persons have lived and worked in the shadow of the Malvern Hills. One of the earliest, William

Langland, has already been mentioned.

The giant amongst those associated with the area must be Edward Elgar. A native of Worcester, he lived in Malvern for many years from 1889. Here he wrote *The Dream of Gerontius* and "Enigma" Variations. His music seems to be so evocative of the area that the label "Elgar Country" has been coined. His birthplace museum is at nearby Lower Broadheath, and his simple grave can be found at St Wulstans RC church at Malvern Wells. His memory, and that of frequent visitor to the town, George Bernard Shaw, lives on in the annual Malvern Festival.

Jenny Lind (the Swedish Nightingale) spent her last years at Wynds Point (British Camp) and Paul Roget, of Thesaurus fame, was buried in Malvern in 1869. Even today the famous resort and reside here, the most recent being the violinist Nigel Kennedy. Fortunately, the less privileged can also enjoy the benefits of living in or visiting this wonderful part of the country.

LIST OF WALKS

B1:	MALVERN TOWN	3.0km	2m
B2:	WORCESTERSHIRE BEACON	6.5km	4m
B3:	NORTH OF MALVERN	5.5km	3½m
B4:	THE CENTRAL RIDGE	9.0km	5½m
B5:	HEREFORDSHIRE BEACON	11.0km	7m
B6:	THE CRADLEY BROOK	6.0km	4m
B7:	RAGGED STONE AND CHASE END HILLS	6.5km	4m

MALVERN HILLS WALKS

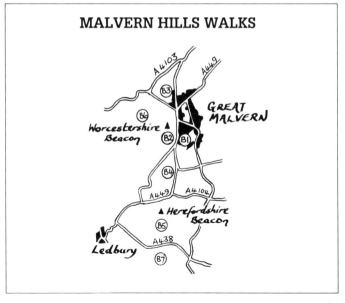

WALK B1:

Malvern Town

Distance:	3km (2m)
Map:	None required
Start Point:	Great Malvern Railway Station, GR 783457
Public Transport:	By rail on Birmingham/Abergavenny line, or direct from Paddington
Refreshments:	Pubs and cafes in the town centre and at the station

A town walk might imply dirty streets thronged with shoppers and air thick with petrol fumes. Not so for this walk! Great Malvern is a storehouse of High Victorian architecture, some Classical, some Gothic, set amongst tree-lined avenues and a backcloth of those marvellous hills. As a prelude to ascending Worcestershire Beacon (Walk B2) or in its own right this is a town walk with a difference.

It is entirely appropriate that the walk should start from the railway station, for this would have been the point at which so many of those Victorian visitors commenced their exploration. The station itself is a gem. A particular feature is the array of cast iron columns, betopped by gaily painted foliage, even "conkers". Look for the stone dog clambering over the roof of the parcels office - and some say that the Victorians were stuffy!

From the forecourt of the station go left, across the junction with Tibberton Road onto Clarence Road, where go right. Here is our first glimpse of those imposing Victorian mansions, their large plots so carefully defined by the original landowners but now often sub-divided to permit the erection of dwellings of inferior architectural merit. The magnificent trees are also a legacy of those patricians.

Turn left onto Albert Road South. Where Woodshears Road is joined take the footpath ahead. Here is one of Malvern's remaining gas lamps, removed in the name of progress in other towns which now lament their lack of heritage. Upon rejoining the road go left, and then left again, onto College Road.

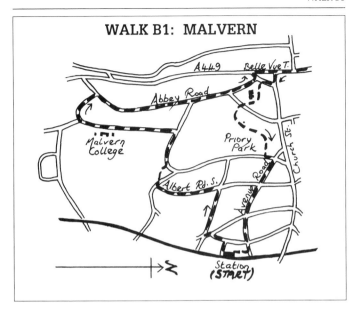

WALK B1: MALVERN

Soon the main buildings of Malvern College are seen on the left. Although these imposing buildings mimic the medieval Decorated style of architecture, when they opened in 1865 they impressed by their advanced internal fitments such as their plumbing.

The road curves round and climbs to join Abbey Road, where go right. The school buildings hereabouts are those of Ellerslie School. Along this road the Scottish Baronial rubs shoulders with the neo-Classical - Elmsdale even has a Disneyesque tower. The Baptist church of 1893 is in Early English style. The large block of apartments named Park View was formerly Priessnitz House, built in 1845 by James Wilson, one of the main exponents of the water cure. Wilson had been a student of Vincenz Priessnitz, a pioneer of such hydropathic remedies.

Continue ahead towards the Abbey Gateway. The Gateway was constructed in the fifteenth century at the time the church itself was being rebuilt, but was heavily restored in the nineteenth century. The gates themselves have long since vanished, although parts of

93

the gateposts remain. The small window inside the arch on the left enabled the gatekeeper to check visitors before allowing admission.

The Gateway now houses the Malvern Museum, which in a small space contrives to trace the history of the town, complete with the early days of radar development.

Pass through the Gateway. On your right the vibrant Gothic of the greengrocers and butchers makes a colourful sight in summer. Cross the road in front of the post office and climb by the sloping bus shelter. Pause before crossing the main Worcester Road. To your left the Mount Pleasant Hotel is one of the earlier hotels in the town. Built around 1730 it precedes the height of the water cure by at least a century. Now cross the road and go right. This is Belle Vue Terrace with a number of interesting shops, notably Manders' pharmacy, with its splendid portico with brass Ionic columns, and still retaining many of the old internal fitments (note also the door handle). In view ahead and to the right is the prow of the Barclays Bank building. It was constructed around 1820 as the Royal Library and Coburg Baths, with reading room, circulating library, music room, billiard room and a bazaar selling a variety of goods. This rapidly became the social centre of the developing town.

Continue to the Unicorn Inn - the oldest in the town centre, originating in the sixteenth century if not earlier. Cross St Ann's Road (linking with Walk B2) and cross to the Foley Arms at the zebra crossing. The central block of the hotel was built in 1810, with later extensions. Bear right down steep Church Street and cross to the post office, then go down the alley on the left to the Priory Church.

Some remnants of the original Norman church, such as the nave piers, the base of the tower and the narrow south aisle can be seen, but this is essentially a fifteenth-century building. From the outside the eye is caught by the warm and colourful stonework - green and red sandstones with oolitic limestone for the finer work. The years have taken their toll but refurbishment has enhanced the building's vigour.

The medieval stained glass is probably second only to York Minster, much dating from the period 1440 to 1500. The range of carving on the misericords should also be examined. These are the ledges under the seats, against which the monks could lean when the seats were tipped up. Ten represent months of the year, others are humorous or grotesque. There are also over 1,000 encaustic tiles, their colours fixed in local kilns.

Before leaving this fine example of Perpendicular architecture, also note the Knotsford monument in the chantry in St Anne's Chapel - this is best seen from the choir.

Outside, turn right and follow the path down through the churchyard, past the east end of the church to emerge in front of the Winter Gardens complex, the focal point of the annual Festival and many other events. To the right is the entry to Priory Park, through which our route leads. Head past the pocket handkerchief tree (Davidia involucrata) towards the bandstand and cross the bridge. Pass between the exuberant Victorian Gothic of Priory Park Mansion (council offices since 1925) and the arid modernity of the Splash, to Priory Road.

Go left, then right onto Avenue Road. Just before returning to the station have a look at the main Girl's College building. It was designed by Elmslie, who was also the architect of the station buildings, as the Imperial Hotel. At the time of its opening it was the only hotel in England lit by incandescent gas and even had its own covered entrance to the station.

WALK B2:
Worcestershire Beacon

Distance:	6.5km (4m)
Map:	OS 1:25,000 Pathfinder 1018, Great Malvern
Start Point:	St Ann's Road, Great Malvern, GR 775461
Public Transport:	Worcester (and Birmingham) to Hereford rail and bus services
Refreshments:	Plentiful pubs and cafes in Great Malvern. St Ann's Well cafe

Worcestershire Beacon is the highest point of the Malvern Hills, standing over its largest settlement. It is inevitable that it should

WALK B2

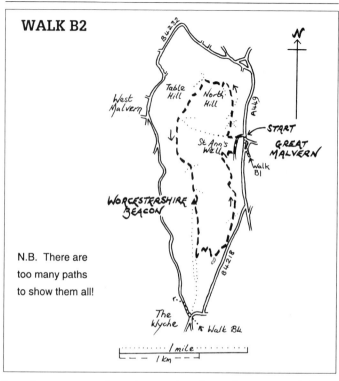

N.B. There are too many paths to show them all!

have become an extremely popular place of resort, receiving a procession of visitors on most days of the year. From some points it is possible to reach the summit within ten minutes of a public road, but this is to miss much of the beauty of the area. This walk takes a less direct route, allowing for leisurely contemplation of the panoramas available.

Walk up St Ann's Road, continuing ahead along Happy Valley where the road bends sharply left. Take a path contouring off to the right opposite Valley House. Ignore crossing paths, and this grassy trod will lead you to a better path, where bear right. This path passes

Looking down on Tintern Abbey

The Round House on The Kymin
Llandogo

under the outcrops of Ivyscar Rocks. These are formed of microdiorite, a form of dolerite, which began life as a molten intrusion into the rocks then still deep underground. Take a path leading upwards to the left, keeping close under the outcrops.

Zigzag upwards - all the time the views have been changing, now Worcester and the Ankerdine Hills are well in view - perhaps further if it is a clear day. Ignore inferior paths leading off and join a better path. Although Worcestershire Beacon is in clear sight ahead, we turn right to join Lady Howard de Walden Drive. The good lady paid for many footpaths and other visitor facilities on the hills during the nineteenth century.

The Drive curves round the nose of the hills, with the gigantic quarries of North Malvern gouged out below. End Hill comes into view, with a broad grassy track coming up the valley on the right. At this point go left, between North and Table Hills - detour to either (or both) to admire the landscape unfolding to east and west. Descend, keeping Worcestershire Beacon (almost due south) in your sights.

Around here there is a veritable profusion of paths - if the visibility is reasonable then choose your own route - otherwise cross Lady Howard de Walden Drive again as it circles round and continue over or just below Sugarloaf Hill.

Join the main tourist path which keeps to the eastern side of the Beacon, almost to the summit at 425m (1,394ft). Here is the usual triangulation column, also an excellent topograph to assist you in identifying the features you can see. A cafe long stood just below the summit, until destroyed by fire - the terrace still remains.

When you have drunk your fill of the views head off to the south, perhaps initially along the remains of the Shire Ditch (see Walk B4 for details). Pinnacle Hill and distinctive, offset Herefordshire Beacon are ahead, with May Hill beyond. Keep to the easternmost path as you descend to find a path to the left, leading off amidst stunted silver birch trees.

The path zigzags down to Earnslaw Quarry, once an eyesore, now a beauty spot with a shallow pool. A path goes off to the left, opposite the quarry entrance, towards Wyche Road. Don't venture quite as far as the road, but take another path leading ahead. This climbs a little. Ignore a crossing path - between the trees is a fine view of the Priory Church.

Contour round to St Ann's Well. Here you can sample some pure Malvern water, in the room next to the cafe.

A tarmac track wends its way down to St Ann's Road where go left, then right, to return to the start point.

WALK B3:

North of Malvern

Distance:	5.5km (3¹/₂m)
Map:	OS 1:25,000 Pathfinder 1018, Great Malvern
Start Point:	Worcestershire Way car park, Cowleigh Road, Malvern, GR 766476
Public Transport:	Malvern to Ledbury bus runs on West Malvern Road
Refreshments:	None on route, but New Inn, Storridge and The Lamb at West Malvern are nearby

A short walk through the wooded hills to the north of the main Malvern range. Without great exertion it allows varying perspectives of the Hills and further afield, with pleasant immediate surroundings. It concludes with a short stretch of the Worcestershire Way.

The information board in the car park explains that the Worcestershire Way leads from here to Kingsford Country Park in the north-west of the county, a journey of some 58km (36m). We are going in the opposite direction, out of the car park, left, and then almost immediately up some steps on the right. These bring you out on Old Hollow, even this short climb opening out the views over the nearby hills and the Severn Plain.

Go right, climbing steadily, but then take the road to the right, signed to the West Malvern Field Centre. Pass between the buildings of the Centre, and then cross two stiles on the right, just after a gateway and before a mobile home. Continue along the wood side and down the hill to a stile in the right-hand corner of the field.

Turn right, go through a gate, and then over a bridge which

spans the Whippets Brook. Continue uphill, through another gate, and keep climbing into the woodland. First turn to look back at Table Hill and Worcestershire Beacon. The entrance is at first being masked by shrubs, but then a good path leads on. At the top of the ridge bear right on another path. Keep right at a fork to follow the woodland edge, looking out over Cradley.

The path re-enters the wood amidst neglected coppice, then passes across the top of a pasture and returns into the wood. In a dip near a disused quarry is a crossing path - go right to leave the wood and drop past Whitman's Hill Farm to the road. Cross to the minor road to Crumpton Hill, past a farm shop which sells its own brand of cider.

Once over the summit you find the little hamlet, half way through which a path is signed to the right. Obey, and then make towards the corner of the wood on the left. Keep to this line until the far corner of the field, to join the Worcestershire Way at a footbridge.

Cross over and now just follow the waymarks along the side of an orchard. The Way bears right, to recross the Whippets Brook, along the side of a wood, and thus to the top of a little ridge. From

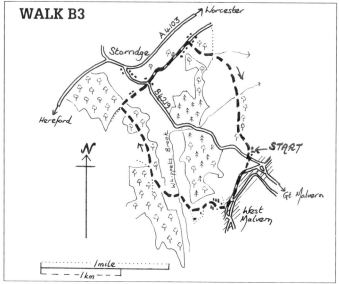

here is a prime view of the Malvern Hills. It is now a simple matter to descend to the start point.

WALK B4:

The Central Ridge

Distance:	9km (5$^{1}/_{2}$m)
Map:	OS 1:25,000 Pathfinder 1018, Great Malvern, or The Malvern Hills, 1:10,000, available locally
Start Point:	Brockhill Road, Colwall, GR 758430
Public Transport:	Colwall BR station (Worcester-Hereford line); Ledbury-Great Malvern bus route; British Camp accessible by bus from Birmingham
Refreshments:	Malvern Hills Hotel; The Wyche Inn; tea rooms at The Wyche

With lofty Worcestershire Beacon on one side and characterful Herefordshire Beacon on the other one might expect this intermediate section of the Malvern Hills to be dull and neglected. Not a bit of it! Although gained with minimal effort the views from the ridge are hardly less inspiring than those from greater heights, and the approach from Colwall and the return have sufficient twists and turns to maintain interest.

From Brockhill Road return to Walwyn Road and turn left. Shortly take Broadwood Drive to the right. This curves round to a gate, passing over the western portal of the 1,433m railway tunnel under the hills. Continue along a gently rising terrace path, and then through open oak woods, to a track and so to the road at Evendine. Now go left.

Turn right along the path signed at Upper House. At the field gate bear slightly right to a protruding field corner, then along the field side towards a footbridge. Continue over further stiles before climbing to the road at British Camp, by the Malvern Hills Hotel.

Now turn briefly left and then cross the road. The path climbs away from the road, but bear right at the point where it threatens to descend rapidly.

Along here is a plaque to Sir Barry Jackson who lived at nearby Black Hill. He was responsible for the Malvern Festival, the first of which was held in 1929, initially a celebration of the work of Edward

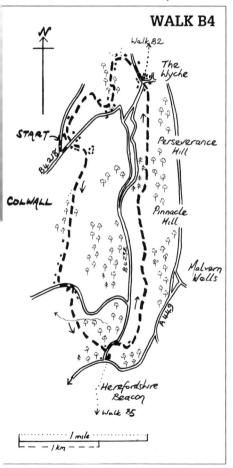

Elgar and George Bernard Shaw. Over the rise behind the plaque is Wynd's Point, where the Swedish Nightingale, Jenny Lind, spent her last years.

The path bends to join the main ridge, with the Worcester-shire countryside spread out below. Simply follow the ridge, either along its very spine or the paths which contour below the crest. The remains of the Shire Ditch, or the Red Earl's Dyke, are to be found at the highest points. Built by Sir Gilbert de Clare in 1287-91, it was the result of a dispute between the Earl and the Bishop of Hereford. Supposedly it was constructed such that deer could leap from the Herefordshire side on to Sir Gilbert's land,

The Central Ridge, looking south from near The Wyche

but not in the opposite direction.

The ridge has a number of tops along its length, starting with Black Hill North at 308m (1,010ft). Pinnacle Hill at 357m (1,173ft) is higher than Herefordshire Beacon, and the last major top is the aptly-named Perseverance Hill at 325m (1,066ft). All the while the panorama is subtly changing, especially as the urban sprawl of Malvern itself comes into view below.

Eventually the descent to the Wyche cutting has to be made. This was for long the crossing of the ancient Salt Way from Droitwich, but the cutting itself was made in about 1840.

Initially take Beacon Road in the direction of West Malvern, but then turn down The Purlieu, still in the tracks of the Salt Way. Bear left as the track does a U-turn to enter woodland, with Herefordshire Beacon in full view ahead. The path becomes quite gloomy as it descends.

At a gate move towards the third opening on the right, signed for The Ryelands, but then cross a stile and bear along the field side to the right. At the next stile a very specific sign urges you to keep to the left of the stream as it bends to the left. After the next stile keep as close to the left as possible, and then you will need to be alert to another stile on the left, swapping from one driveway to another. Go right to the road - on your left is The Winnings, once the home of Stephen Ballard, one of the founders of the Malvern Hills Conservators, who also engineered the first railway tunnel under the hills.

At the road go right, passing Old Court Nurseries, home of the National Michaelmas Daisy Collection. Brockhill Road is then to your right.

WALK B5:

Herefordshire Beacon

Distance:	11km (7m)
Map:	OS 1:25,000 Pathfinder 1041, Ledbury and Much Marcle, or The Malvern Hills, 1:10,000, available locally
Start Point:	Hollybush, GR 766368
Public Transport:	Bus services between Great Malvern and both Ledbury and Birmingham stop at British Camp
Refreshments:	None on route. Plume of Feathers and Robin Hood inns on B4208 at Castlemorton

Each year thousands of visitors climb Herefordshire Beacon from the car park at the summit of the British Camp pass, a simple ascent rewarded by some of the finest views to be found anywhere. This walk takes a more subtle and lengthier approach of diverse and contrasting images such as a cave, two Iron Age camps and an obelisk, to create a wholly satisfying excursion.

From the small parking area at Hollybush bear to the rear of the church but to the left of Golden Valley into which small farms and cottages comfortably nestle. The path leads gently down to the Mill Pond, often with Jacob sheep present. The area around the pond is a popular picnic resort.

At the field corner go left, and keep reasonably close to the hedge. We are here on Hollybed Common. Over the years much of the common land to the east of the Malvern Hills has been enclosed and cultivated, that which remains being too infertile to be worth enclosing. This adds to its potential for flora and fauna - such rarities as the tubular water dropwort, if you know what to look for - and a wide range of moorland and wetland birds can also be seen.

The path passes between two cottages and along a green track, the Malverns marching stride-by-stride at your shoulder, until the road is reached. Here go left. At the little road junction take a track

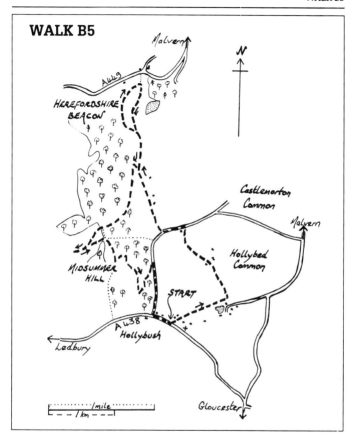

WALK B5

to the right, rising gently along the flank of the hills, to the crest of the ridge, at the Silurian Pass. The Pass is so-called because sandstones of Silurian age (about 435 to 395 million years old) are here set into the much older Precambrian rocks from which most of the hills are formed. Contour ahead, passing Clutters Cave, hacked out of volcanic rocks. If Clutter was a giant, as is reputed, he must have been an economy size one. More plausibly this was a hermit's cell.

Take the path to the left which climbs, paved with Malvernian stone, over to the Herefordshire flank of the Hills before ascending to the summit of Herefordshire Beacon. From here it is possible to survey the impressive earthworks which extend over thirty-two acres. Probably first started around 500 years BC one can only marvel at the organisation and effort which could create the impressive defences which give the Hill its distinctive profile. It is estimated that at its peak between 1,500 and 2,000 people would have permanently resided within these ramparts, and one cannot envy the Romans their task in subduing such tribes. As from all lofty points on the Malverns the views are breathtaking. On one side is the Severn Plain and the Cotswolds, to the other the Black Mountains and the Sugar Loaf, with the long line of the Malverns ahead and astern.

The descent to the north-east is down a clearly worn path. After a long flight of steps take a path to the right which contours above the late nineteenth-century reservoir. The path rejoins our outward route, but it is possible to walk further to the left on Broad Down, and follow the Shire Ditch (see Walk B4). At the Silurian Pass take a path descending sharply to the right through a tunnel of bushes, to join a track, where go left. The track swings along the slopes of Swinyard Hill and into Gullet Wood.

On leaving the wood carry on towards the obelisk. Built of oolitic limestone from the Cotswolds, it was erected in 1812 to commemorate members of the Somers family of Eastnor Castle.

Return down the main track, but turn right at the gate to The Gullet. After passing Midsummer Cottage in a hollow on the left, take a path rising up to the ridge, and continue climbing to the summit of Midsummer Hill at 284m (932ft). In the ownership of the National Trust, here stood another Iron Age hill fort. Excavated in part between 1965 and 1970 it was discovered that the ramparts had been faced with sandstone from nearby Bronsil and limestone from Coombegreen Common to the east. The entrance had seventeen sets of gateposts between 470 BC and AD 48. Nowadays the only structure is a bus shelter (well that's what the wind shelter looks like).

Retreat slightly, and drop to the head of the valley on the right to ascend to the twin summit of Hollybush Hill. By this lower summit a path goes off to the left (east), falling quite rapidly to a minor road. Go to the right to rejoin the A438, the start point then being to the left.

WALK B6:

The Cradley Brook

Distance:	6km (4m)
Map:	OS 1:25,000 Pathfinder 1018, Great Malvern
Start Point:	Stifford's Bridge, opposite the Seven Stars on A4103, GR 734491
Public Transport:	Worcester to Cradley bus route
Refreshments:	Red Lion and Seven Stars Inns, Stifford's Bridge; Cliffe Arms, Mathon

The Cradley Brook flows through a gentle valley on its way to join the Leigh Brook and thence the River Teme, these shallow slopes contrasting with the Malvern Hills, which rear up in the background. The Brook links two villages, Mathon and Cradley, with field paths which cross and recross this watery umbilical cord. An easy and pleasant stroll for a summer's evening or a winter's afternoon results.

At Stifford's Bridge a kissing gate opposite the Seven Stars leads into a field. The scene is distinctly pastoral, with sheep safely grazing alongside the willow and alder-lined brook. The seeds from the latter are often carried downstream to germinate in the waterside mud. Former uses of the wood included clog soles, and poles for charcoal used in the manufacture of gunpowder.

After a house turn right down a tarmac lane. Enter the yard of Wold Mill and go up the flight of steps on the left, just after the house, to a pedestrian gate. It may feel as if you are on someone's garden, but it is the right of way. Cross the field to a stile just to the left of a cottage. Across the lane is a half-hidden fence stile, over which is a good path. This leads on to the road at the side of the school.

Turn left, and go up the lane to the church from the war

memorial. The timber-framed lychgate is of the sixteenth century and the church itself has a late Norman chancel and nave doorways, the tower being built around 1200. In the north wall of the tower is a fragment of a Saxon frieze. Further along the lane is the gem of the fifteenth-century former school, now used as a parish hall. It has moulded bressumers and dragon beams, which sound very grand! (The former run horizontally, supporting the joists at the back of the overhang, the latter are horizontal members running diagonally from an internal cross-beam to the corner post.)

The path continues half-right, across a stream, and then into Lumbridge Hill Wood. In summer "weeds" such as rosebay willow herb and ragwort form a colourful garden along here. Follow the stream as it does a U turn, but take a new footbridge to the right to leave the wood. Go through a gate and then keep the fieldside on your right to a track and another gate. Once through this gate bear

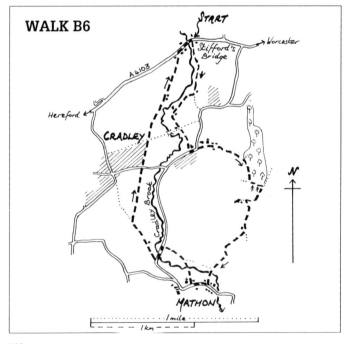

WALK B6

left, not entering the farm ahead. Now pass through an isolated cottage garden and walk along the access lane.

Downhill and on the left a stile leads to a footbridge over the Brook and so into Mathon. The village has the dubious distinction of having a weed with a daisy-like flower and an unpleasant smell named after it.

A short detour to the left finds the Cliffe Arms. Our route goes instead to the right, and then right again just before the church of St John the Baptist, which has early Norman fragments such as doorways with plain tympana above.

The path crosses a field and then Cradley Brook again on its way to another track. Go left this time to the road. Left again, and once more over the Brook. Now go right, down a track, and then over a stile just left of a house.

Follow the fieldside over a little stream, and then curve round to a gate. There are fine views along virtually the entire Malvern range from here. Once through the gate go over the stile ahead and plough on to the road. Cross over and walk along the lane, part way up the valley side.

Cross another road and follow the fieldside. At a stile keep just left of the houses, over another stile and through a gate. At the end of the field the stile is hidden away down the bank on the right. Soon the road is regained, where go right to return to the start point - although two pubs lie in the way!

WALK B7:
Ragged Stone and Chase End Hills

Distance:
                           6.5km (4m)

Map: OS 1:25,000 Pathfinder 1041, Ledbury and Much Marcle

Start Point: Hollybush (A438), GR 769369

Public Transport: None readily accessible

Refreshments: None on route

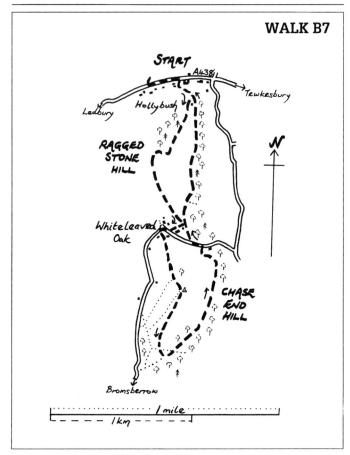

WALK B7

START

A438

Tewkesbury

Ledbury

Hollybush

RAGGED
STONE
HILL

Whiteleaved
Oak

CHASE
END
HILL

Bromsberrow

1 mile

1 km

N

The final undulations of the Malvern Hills manifest themselves as Ragged Stone and Chase End Hills. Lower than, and detached from, the main ridge, they tend to be less well trodden, and this adds to their quiet charms. Attractive at any time of year, but especially in autumn, this short walk can also be added to Walk B5 to form an absorbing introduction to the southern Malverns.

Walk down the road from the car park, in the direction of

Tewkesbury. Shortly before the telephone kiosk take a track to the right, which curves to the left as it gains height. Immediately after a gate take the path to the right, which heads directly (and hence quite steeply) to one of the twin summits of Ragged Stone Hill.

I suppose I should have warned you that the hill is cursed. Apparently a monk at nearby Little Malvern Priory lapsed in his vow of chastity, and as a penance had to climb Ragged Stone Hill each day on his hands and knees. He was supposed to pray when he reached the summit, but one day instead he cursed the hill and all upon whom its shadow should fall. Victims are said to include Cardinal Wolsey and William Huskisson MP - the latter killed in an accident whilst Stephensons Rocket was being tested.

Still, it's too late to worry about such things now. Admire the views over the Severn Vale, with Bredon Hill prominent and then traverse to the higher summit at 254m (833ft). Views open out to the west with Eastnor Castle especially prominent when clothed in its fiery autumnal mantle of Virginia Creeper. Now descend the ridge until confronted by a token of civilisation in the shape of a garage.

Go right to join the tarmac road. This is Whiteleaved Oak - a lovely name for a delectable cluster of original and restored dwellings in one of the most tranquil spots imaginable. The hamlet straddles the boundaries of the Three Counties - Worcestershire, Gloucestershire and Herefordshire.

Proceed right and immediately after the road bends left take an often muddy track on the left at the side of Cider Mill Cottage. Soon you are on the open fellside with a stiff little climb to the triangulation column at the summit of Chase End Hill (once known as Gloucestershire Beacon). At a height of 191m (626ft) the views are particularly open to the south, to the Cotswolds, May Hill (an upturned pudding bowl with a clump of trees on the top) and on a clear day a glimpse of the Severn Estuary.

Continue south along the ridge, descending to a clear crossing track, where go left. Pass through light woodland until meeting the road, where bear left. After about 30m take the path ascending through woodland on the right, to emerge once more at the garage guarding Ragged Stone Hill. This time go right along another pleasant woodland track which in due course will return you to the A438 at Hollybush.

THE WYE VALLEY

INTRODUCTION

The River Wye rises high on the lonely slopes of Plynlimon, in remote mid-Wales. Its source is only a short distance from that of the Severn, which it eventually meets at Chepstow after a journey of some 248km (154 miles). It enters Herefordshire just outside the border town of Hay-on-Wye, and then traverses the plain towards Hereford. It then changes direction, from west-east to north-south.

For the purposes of this book the Wye Valley starts where the valley sides steepen after this change of direction. Initially the slopes are those of the Woolhope Dome. The river then passes the town of Ross-on-Wye, before its meanders become hugely exaggerated loops. The beauty spot of Symonds Yat marks the start of the romantically picturesque gorge which the river has carved past Monmouth, and so to Chepstow.

Geology

The geology of the southern part of this area is indivisible from that of the adjoining Forest of Dean, and is covered in the introduction to that section of this book. Once upon a time the Wye flowed over the surface of what is now the Forest. Then, during the Ice Ages, the sea level fell. The Wye continued along the same route, cutting through the old rocks. We now have those old meanders (some since abandoned) superimposed on the modern landscape.

One of the most fascinating areas is that of the Woolhope Dome. Here the Silurian inlier has been forced into an anticline, a fold - in this case almost a bubble, with the south-western slope dipping more steeply than the north-eastern. Other complications include the variety of strata, notably limestones and shales, but also mudstones and siltstones. The whole area is heavily faulted, giving rise to an intimate landscape of ridges and valleys.

Natural History

The valley sides, often of Devonian sandstone, but with impressive limestone crags in many places, support a wealth of wildlife. Here is the best selection of native British trees to be found anywhere in the wild - see if you can recognise all sixty-five on the walks in this book! The most prolific are easily identified - oak, hazel and birch.

The Wye Valley woods support a varied flora, particularly before the broadleaves shade out the ground storey. From early spring the wood anemone, celandine, primrose, violet and dog's mercury are succeeded by bluebells, wild garlic (ramsons) and early purple orchid.

As usual the limestone carries an impressive flora, including bee orchid, blue fleabane, madder, autumn gentian, pencilled cranesbill and lady's tresses. A rich variety of mosses is also to be found. The Great Doward (Walk C8) is a botanical storehouse - over 130 species of flower have been recorded on the Leeping Stocks reserve of the Herefordshire Nature Trust. These include white helleborine, gromwell, bee orchid and meadow saffron. Nearby, the Lord's Wood quarry features evening primrose, ploughman's spikenard, wood sage and St John's wort.

Across the river is the ecological reserve of Lady Park Wood, established by the Forestry Commission to study unmanaged woodland. Here can be found the dormouse, yellow-necked woodmouse, blackcap and garden warbler. Nesting peregrine falcons are a speciality at Coldwell Rocks, and can be viewed from Symonds Yat Rock. Elsewhere on the limestone cliffs jackdaws and kestrels may be seen. Coppet Hill (Walk C7) is frequented by buzzards and the lesser whitethroat.

History

King Arthur's Cave (Walk C8) has revealed the remains of hyena, mammoth, woolly rhino, cave bear and beaver. It was occupied by man during the Stone Age through to the Bronze Age. Harold's Stones at Trelleck (Walk C15) date from the Bronze Age. The Queen Stone at Huntsham, near Goodrich, was allegedly erected around 2000 BC. It has deeply incised grooves on four sides and there is evidence of fire on the top surface.

The above point to considerable early human activity in the area. Iron Age hill forts are, by contrast, few in number. There is one on Little Doward and a good example on Capler Camp (Walk C4). Roman times have left more archaeological information. Ariconium, under Bollitree and Bury Hill near Ross, was one centre. Coins, pottery and smelting pits have been found here. A Roman villa has been discovered at Huntsham and a horde of fourth-century coins at nearby Bishopswood. The Silures under Caratacus harried the Romans mercilessly for 30 years - one battle allegedly took place at The Slaughter (Walk C8). A Roman road, Watling Street West, runs from Chepstow to Monmouth via Trelleck.

One of the most remarkable structures to remain is Offa's Dyke. From Sedbury near Chepstow it runs high above the eastern valley of the Wye to just south of Monmouth. A fuller description of this eighth-century defensive work is given in Appendix 1.

We are here in the neighbourhood of Archenfield, an area bordered by the Rivers Wye, Monnow and Worm, which retained its independence from the Saxons for 500 years until overthrown by the Welsh and then the Normans.

The Normans left their mark along the length of the valley. Whilst little remains of the castle of Wilton (Walk C6), Goodrich (Walk C7) is almost a textbook example of the evolving art of military defence. There are also traces of this defensive chain at Monmouth and St Briavel's (Walk C14). The outstanding example of the genre is at Chepstow (Walk C16).

One might expect a richness of ecclesiastical buildings. The pride of the valley is Tintern Abbey, a Cistercian foundation of 1131. This gem of a monastery may be visited on Walk C12. St Briavel's and Fownhope also have Norman elements remaining, but other than this the most impressive churches are of a later period, notably Newland (Walk C11).

Industrial History

Perhaps surprisingly, the Wye Valley was once a major industrial centre. The river itself was the transport artery for the area, evolving a special kind of cargo boat, the trow. Iron, cider, corn and oak bark were shipped across the estuary to Bristol.

Tintern and the Angidy Valley were particularly associated with metalworking - the country's first water-powered wire-drawing works were founded here in 1566. Initially brass wire was produced, then iron-wire, especially used for wool-carding. A charcoal blast furnace and three forges were to follow - the remains of the ironworks at the head of the Angidy Valley have been restored and are now accessible.

The seventeenth-century Coed Ithel blast furnace, the wire-works and later paper mills of the Whitebrook Valley and the tinplate works of Redbrook are now just memories. Redbrook had been an iron-smelting centre since the early seventeenth century, and later turned to smelting copper imported from Cornwall. Even Symonds Yat had an iron forge - the Earl of Shrewsbury had built a blast furnace at nearby Whitchurch around 1575, the forge soon following. A major forge was built at New Weir in 1684, surviving until the early nineteenth century, by which time the industry was in decline.

The area was later served by the Ross and Monmouth Railway (opened in 1873), and the Wye Valley Railway from Monmouth to Chepstow of 1876. Both lines are long since closed, but Tintern station has been resurrected as a most successful visitor centre (Walk C14).

The Wye Tours

The Reverend William Gilpin is credited with being the author of the cult of the picturesque. He developed his theories out of classical ideas of landscape beauty. Artists such as Lorraine, Poussin and Wilson interpreted landscapes in a stylised way. Gilpin wrote books such as his 1782 tome *Observations of the River Wye*. Nowadays we might stop at points such as Symonds Yat to admire the view. Gilpin went a step further, prescribing certain viewing points which met his criteria, the scene to be viewed in a mirror! He thought Tintern Abbey would be improved by the judicious use of a mallet, if anyone had so dared.

Tours by boat from Ross gained in popularity, at $1^1/_2$ guineas per trip. Turner visited the Abbey in 1792, and drew it a number of times. The Napoleonic Wars meant that many who would once have undertaken the Grand Tour of Europe now sought beauty and culture in their own country. Other visitors included William Wordsworth, who penned "Lines written above Tintern Abbey" following a visit. At Goodrich he supposedly met the little girl who inspired "Now We Are Seven".

Angling

The Wye must rank as Mecca for many anglers. Elvers are caught below Ross in some quantity. Minnows, stone loach, gudgeon, dace, roach, perch, chub, pike, tench and occasional grayling or trout are to be found in the river, but its fame arises because it is honoured by the presence of the regal salmon. Once exceedingly plentiful, the construction of weirs and the use of nets dramatically reduced numbers. The Wye Board of Conservators was formed in 1866 to conserve fish stocks - prohibition of netting in the freshwater Wye from 1908 was one of the essential steps.

The salmon spawns in November or December, the eggs hatching three or four months later. After two years in the river the young migrate to the sea during the spring. They return to spawn, having grown considerably. The fish can grow to be over 13.6kg (30lb) although there are less large fish nowadays.

Famous fishermen include Alderman Robert Pashley of Kerne Bridge. In 1932 he caught fifty-three salmon in $4^1/_2$ days. In 1936 he caught 678 fish, grossing 4,909kg (10,822lb), a world record. Over a career of fifty years he is credited with having landed no less than 10,237 salmon. Today's fishermen tend to be more modest in their ambitions - between 1,000 and 8,000 fish are caught each year.

The Wye from The Seven Sisters rocks. (Walk C8)

LIST OF WALKS

C1:	HAUGH WOOD	11.0km	7m
C2:	THE MARCLE RIDGE	10.0km	6m
C3:	SELLACK, KING'S CAPLE AND HOARWITHY	8.0km	5m
C4:	CAPLER CAMP	13.5km	8$\frac{1}{2}$m
C5:	PENYARD HILL	11.5km	7m
C6:	ROSS-ON-WYE	5.5km	3$\frac{1}{2}$m
C7:	COPPET HILL	11.5km	7m
C8:	SYMONDS YAT	7.5 or 8.5km	5 or 5$\frac{1}{2}$m
C9:	BUCKHOLT WOOD AND WELSH NEWTON COMMON	13.0km	8m
C10:	MONMOUTH AND THE KYMIN	11.5km	7m
C11:	REDBROOK AND NEWLAND	9.0km	5$\frac{1}{2}$m
C12:	TINTERN ABBEY AND THE DEVIL'S PULPIT	7.0km	4$\frac{1}{2}$m
C13:	THE NARTH	5.0km	3m
C14:	BROCKWEIR TO BIGSWEIR	14.0km	8$\frac{1}{2}$m
C15:	TRELLECK CURIOSITIES	2.0km	1$\frac{1}{2}$m
C16:	WINTOUR'S LEAP	10.0km	6$\frac{1}{2}$m
C17:	WYND CLIFF	12.0km	7$\frac{1}{2}$m

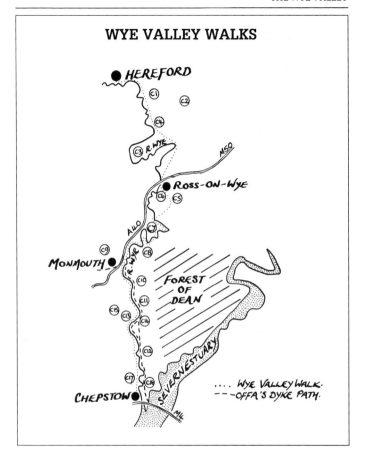

WYE VALLEY WALKS

HEREFORD

C1 C2

C4

C3 R. WYE

M50

ROSS-ON-WYE

C6 C5

A40

C7

C9 C8

MONMOUTH

R. WYE

C10

C11

C15

C14

C12

SEVERN ESTUARY

FOREST OF DEAN

C17 C16

CHEPSTOW

M4

.... WYE VALLEY WALK.
-- -- OFFA'S DYKE PATH.

WALK C1:
Haugh Wood

Distance:	11km (7m)
Map:	OS 1:25,000 Pathfinder 1041, Hereford (South)
Start Point:	Lay-by on Woolhope Road through Mordiford, GR 575373
Public Transport:	Hereford to Fownhope bus service
Refreshments:	Moon Inn, Mordiford

The Woolhope Dome is noted by naturalists for its wealth of wildlife, especially the limestone flora. The countryside is also very attractive, and access has been improved by the Forestry Commission, who own the great swathe of Haugh Wood. The valley of the Pentaloe Brook is particularly pleasant, and routefinding is assisted by the use of parts of no less than four waymarked paths.

From the lay-by walk briefly uphill and take the path on the left signed for the Mordiford Loop Walk. This curves round into a small estate, the path leading off after the third bungalow on the left. Now walk through the charming streamside pastures by the Pentaloe Brook, before joining a track. Leave the track to the right, passing a derelict cottage to enter the wood. Go left.

Take your time over the next section. Keep left at a fork. Around here squirrels forage for hazel nuts in the autumn, and flowers and plants such as teasel, hemp agrimony and fragrant orchid are to be found. After crossing the Brook look for a waymark to the right, to leave the wood alongside the Brook.

Pass through fields and curve to the right. Look for a stile to cross a lane, and follow the Brook until you reach the road in the hamlet of Checkley. Turn right, pass the post office, and walk through the scattered cottages around the common. Now take a tarmac track to the right. Turn right at a junction, then left, over a cattle grid.

Pass a restored half-timbered cottage, after which the path

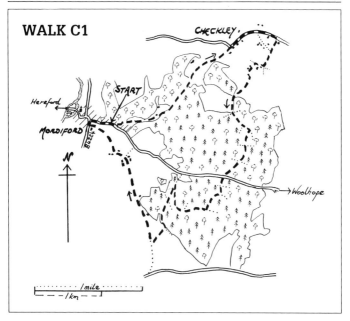

temporarily vanishes. After a derelict barn bear half left through a neglected orchard. Cross a footbridge and follow the field side on the right. Go over a stile and continue alongside the hedge. The path rises to a muddy area between two woods - bear outside the one on the left, to a gate.

You are now in Haugh Wood, a Forestry Commission woodland with public access. Follow the route to the left marked by red-ringed posts. After crossing a stream turn right, uphill, crossing two forestry tracks. Oaks screen the conifer plantations, and clumps of innocuous-looking cow wheat abound. Keep to the left at the car park and picnic area, and then cross the road.

Now cross a forest ride, passing some store buildings. Go right at a fork, still on a forestry track. This curves to the right and another track comes in from the left. You may well catch a glimpse of the shy fallow deer - but not if they see you first! Keep to the track as it bends left, then right. On approaching a barrier take a path doubling back off the main track.

Pass through conifer plantations, crossing first a poor track, then a better one, before curving to the left. The path is here starting to be overgrown by brambles. Finally go through a rickety pedestrian gate on the right to join a lane, where go left.

The lane runs along just outside the wood. At a bend a waymark points across the field to the right, where there is a footbridge over a small stream. Head half left up the hill. Half way up this field is the line of the Wye Valley Walk, where go right.

From now on there are liberal waymarks, over a stile, slightly right to the next one, and so towards the farm of Hope Springs. Pass between the buildings and turn left. At the next group of houses a sunken lane leads off to the right, through some orchards. Turn left, passing the rusty waterwheel of the old mill. Once on the road turn right.

The start point is down the road to the right, but a short detour left is recommended. Here is the fourteenth-century bridge, beneath which the Lugg flows in divided channels, shortly to meet the Wye. Here too are picnic spots, and here once was a dragon, if legend is to be believed. Found and nurtured by a young girl, it soon grew and thrived on farm animals. A condemned man was promised his freedom if he could rid the village of this pest. He hid in a barrel and shot an arrow through a hole, slaying the beast. Unfortunately its dying breath set fire to the barrel and the dragon-slayer also perished.

WALK C2:
The Marcle Ridge

Distance:	10km (6m)
Map:	OS 1:25,000 Pathfinder 1041, Ledbury and Much Marcle
Start Point:	Marcle Ridge car park, GR 631346
Public Transport:	Some Hereford to Fownhope bus services are extended to Woolhope
Refreshments:	The Crown, Woolhope; The Butchers Arms

The Marcle Ridge mimics the loftier Malvern Hills to the north-east, a long ridge looking out on one side over sedate Leadon Vale, and on the other over the delightful confusion of the Woolhope Dome. From the airy vantage point of the ridge one is soon plunged into the intimate landscape of this reclusive area, with lovely scenes at every turn.

From the car park walk briefly uphill and take the stile on the right. Now just follow the ridge, and take in the views - unfortunately partly masked by trees on the west. The Malverns, May Hill and the Cotswolds are all clearly seen. The triangulation point at 231m (758ft) gives cause for a pause to look across the area over which you will soon be walking.

In high winds the area around the television mast is not for the nervous, but the path quickly descends to a sunken lane, where go right. This is a perfectly charming spot, overarched by trees, bedecked in spring by violets, primroses and celandines, with grey squirrels

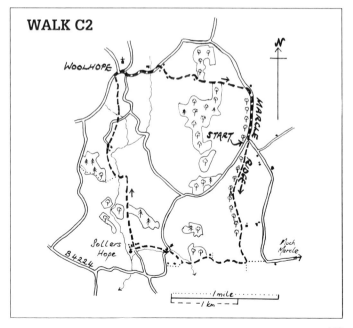

Gatekeeper on guelder rose

scurrying around. Reality returns at some farm buildings, where agility is required to avoid acquiring muddy encrustations.

Daffodils, guelder rose, stinking hellebore or other seasonal flora should restore confidence, the nature of the soil being confirmed by the presence of limekilns. Cross a stream and go over the stile on the right, then cross the field to a gate by the stream. Now follow the stream - the orchard on the opposite bank is festooned with mistletoe and the stream widens to form a pretty pond. At the road go briefly left, then right, by the farm buildings. Keep to the left of the low hill and head for Court Farm.

Sollers Hope is one of those special finds, a charming grouping of buildings reminding one of a long-forgotten age. The name means the hollow of the Solas family, and this is one of the claimed birthplaces of Dick Whittington. The chimney stack to the half-timbered house is as intriguing as its description: "crow-stepped above eaves level and surmounted by two octagonal shafts with trefoil-headed panels on the bases and topped by moulded concave-sided caps".

The nearby church of St Michael's is largely of the fourteenth century, although the windows are mainly of the fifteenth. There is a coffin slab of around 1225 incised with the image of a knight - believed to be a member of the Solas family.

Return to the farm, passing between the house and the farm buildings and bearing left out of the farmyard. Continue ahead, into the next field, moving close to the field boundary on the right. Pass a wood.

Now keep the field boundary to your left until a stile, where go left. Cross a stream, and a little distance along the hedge on your right hand is a stile. Cross this and head towards a little "magpie" cottage, to the left of which a gate leads onto a lane. Follow this past the cottage and the farmstead of Alford's Mill.

On the right a signpost bids you enter a field, through a gate. Keep the hedge on your right but at the corner bear left across the field, with Woolhope in view ahead. Cross a stile, continue ahead and over another stile onto a lane. Climb the stile ahead and bear half right to a footbridge. Now keep the hedge on your left, with the church tower in your sights. The field boundary disappears and then reappears on the right, and when it ends bear left to a stile (just left of a new bungalow). Turn right on the road.

You are now in Woolhope, named after Wuliva, Lady Godiva's sister, who supposedly owned the manor in the eleventh century. There is a modern stained glass window to the sisters in the largely thirteenth-/fourteenth-century church of St George, up the hill to the left. We continue past the Crown Inn, ignoring roads to left and right as the main road drops to The Butcher's Arms.

Just before the inn a lane wends its way uphill to the right. Outcrops and lime kilns confirm that the ridge is of Wenlock limestone. The path follows a woodland edge as it falls into a valley of the softer Elton Beds, before climbing back to the road. Turn right. The highest part of the ridge is formed of the calcareous siltstones and flaggy or silty limestones of the Bringewood Beds. The start point is soon regained.

WALK C3:
Sellack, King's Caple and Hoarwithy

Distance:	8km (5m)
Map:	OS 1:25,000 Pathfinder 1064, Ross-on-Wye (West)
Start Point:	Hoarwithy Bridge, GR 549295
Public Transport:	Ross-Hoarwithy-Hereford bus route
Refreshments:	New Inn, Hoarwithy

Is this walk a celebration of the River Wye, or of three contrasting villages and their churches? The answer has to be, both, for the villages are inextricably linked to the river. The only way to appreciate that relationship, and the beauty of this area is to walk the paths that bind it together.

Cross the recently reconstructed bridge, passing the former toll house on your way towards the village. Take the second road on the right, just along which a flight of steps on the left leads to the unique church of St Catherine. The inspiration came from the Reverend William Poole, who was vicar here for forty-six years. The design was the work of J.P.Seddon. The result is an Italianate church of 1885. It has a four-storey campanile, an arched external cloister walk, and an apse with the "Pantokrator" in gold mosaic on the floor. Other features include the arch of doves and the four Devonshire marble columns.

Return to the road and turn right. Walk in the direction of Ross, passing the New Inn. A short distance after a minor road junction signs for a bridleway and then a footpath are seen on the right. Take the latter, angling uphill. Pass a house and cross a track, then keep the hedge to your right. The path climbs along pleasant upland pastures, with views over the river to King's Caple and beyond.

The path curves to the head of a dry valley and enters a copse. Upon leaving keep right, on a track. Another joins from the right, but keep ahead to the road. Go left, downhill, to cross the main road, and enter a field. Bear right, now along the banks of the Wye.

Here dawdling is forgivable - the river itself glides along during the summer months, although it shows a darker side to its character during winter and spring, when it flows strong and deep, sometimes covering the route you now tread.

In due course bear away from the river towards Sellack church, which is the only one in England dedicated to St Tysilio. The Saint was the son of the King of Powys, and was persecuted by his relatives for choosing the monastic life. Eventually he fled to Brittany, dying at St Suliac in about 650. The church itself has Norman origins, largely obliterated by fourteenth-century rebuilding and a nineteenth-century transept. The east window has fragments of old stained glass, assembled in 1630.

Returning outside, one is struck by the peacefulness of the location. Sometimes words are superfluous in such places, as the epitaph writer evidently thought when he inscribed a cross in the churchyard, to the east of the church, with a hand with an upthrust finger and the solitary word, Gone.

Now return to the river and swing across the suspension

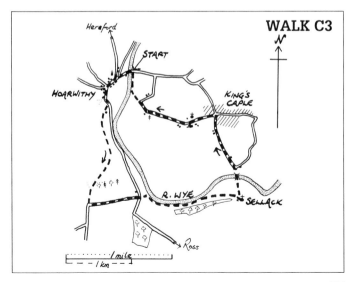

bridge. Take the road uphill to King's Caple. At the crossroads turn left towards the church. On entering the churchyard note the Plague Cross, the reason for the name only becoming obvious when a pit was discovered. In it lay the remains of at least twenty-five people, probably victims of the Black Death of 1348. There are fine views from the churchyard over the valley, looping round from Sellack to Brockhampton.

The church is largely a product of the thirteenth and fourteenth centuries. Many of the bosses in the Lady Chapel are carved with heads, those over the south arch having pagan origins. The pulpit, sounding board and pews are of the seventeenth century. The benefactors' board on the west wall lists the local charities, including the Cake Money. This originated from the will of Thomas More, a vicar of Sellack and King's Caple who died in 1484. Pax Cakes, bearing the words "Peace and Good Neighbourhood", are still given to the congregations of the two parishes, and neighbouring Hentland, every Palm Sunday.

Opposite the churchyard gate is Caple Tump, a mound which was once the motte of a Norman castle. Later it was used for dancing and other festivities. Turn right and follow the road until a sharp right-hand bend, where take the green lane carrying on straight ahead. This bends to return to Hoarwithy Bridge.

WALK C4:

Capler Camp

Distance:	13¹/₂km (8¹/₂m)
Map:	OS 1:25,000 Pathfinder 1040, Hereford (South)
Start Point:	Fownhope Church (please do not park near at times of services)
Public Transport:	Hereford to Fownhope bus service
Refreshments:	Fownhope has 3 pubs
Other Information:	*Guide to All Saints, Brockhampton* (small charge)
	Guide to St Mary's, Fownhope (small charge)

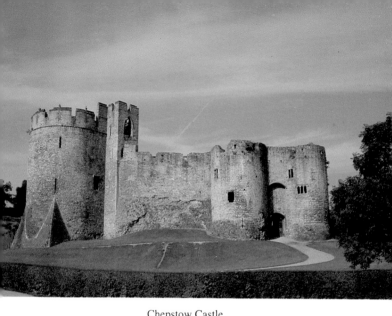

Chepstow Castle

Flaxley Abbey

Soudley Ponds

Looking across the Forest

Lea & Paget's Wood Nature Trail Leaflet,
Herefordshire Naturalist's Trust

It is always a delight to walk around the Woolhope Dome and the Wye Valley and this walk is no exception. Initially on the Wye Valley long distance footpath, it visits the prehistoric fort at Capler Camp, and a unique and captivating thatched church, followed by a walk on the banks of the Wye itself. Interesting woodlands and beautiful views intervene, and the village of Fownhope itself has its own selection of curiosities to detain visitors.

Take the minor road facing the church, opposite the one signed to Capler. Turn left onto Church Croft and at the signboard for Nover Wood Drive take the path on the right. This climbs past the

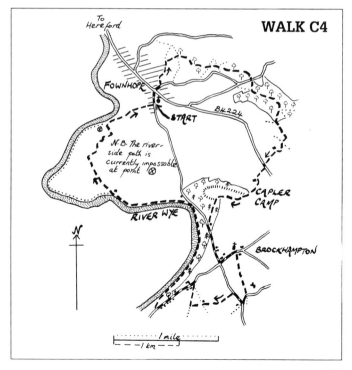

back gardens of a housing estate. After the last house turn off on to another path on the right.

After passing a secluded cottage go left to join the Wye Valley Walk at a viewpoint. Turn right for a wholly delightful stroll along this attractive little ridgetop. In late summer squadrons of gatekeeper butterflies flit around the scarlet berried guelder rose and remnants of honeysuckle, whilst cottages nestle comfortably amidst orchards laden with apples, pears and plums.

One can detour slightly right to the summit of Common Hill for views of the Black Mountains away to the west, but the main route continues to cross a minor road. Go downhill about 50m and turn left onto a crossing path which enters shady Paget's Wood, passing some half-interred lime kilns. The lime stone from the quarry a little further into the wood and a quantity of timber was tipped into a hole at the top of the kiln. After burning the resultant quicklime could be spread on the fields to neutralise acid soils. The wood rests in a valley formed in the Ludlow Shale between a ridge of Wenlock Limestone to the north and one of Aymestry Limestone to the south.

The woodland is still in part coppiced in the traditional manner letting in the light which encourages a diversity of flowers such as orchids. Fallow deer may also be seen.

At a junction of paths follow the Wye Valley Walk main route signs to the right. The numbered signs relate to the nature trail (see above for leaflet). On leaving the wood take care not to go straight on but to go over the stile on the left, passing a derelict cottage, then turning right, downhill. Cross a small stream and then follow the field boundary to the left. At the top of the field go over a stile and then keep right to emerge on a farm track, where go left to join a road. Now go left, then right, still following the Wye Valley Walk waymarks.

Don't stride too boldly down the farm track, for stiles to the left and then the right allow the farmstead to be circumvented. A flight of steps leads to Capler Camp, where bear right, behind a barn, to discover the earthworks of this Iron-Age hill fort. The ramparts are still clearly visible, and offer a perch on which to eat sandwiches and admire the view round from May Hill to Ross-on-Wye. On the southern side of the camp is the dew pond which formed the Camp's water supply.

Brockhampton Church

Keep to the southern side of the Camp, climb a stile, and join a track. Shortly afterwards take a stile on the left with a path leading through a new plantation. Cross another stile to rejoin the wooded track, downhill to the road, where turn left. Almost opposite is a superb viewpoint over the Wye.

Turn left at the junction and shortly the church of All Saints, Brockhampton is seen on the left. So natural are its materials of local red sandstone and thatch, and its design with echoes of traditional themes, that it is rather a shock to discover that it was completed in 1902. The architect was W.R.Lethaby, a product of the arts and crafts movement synonymous with the name of William Morris. Closer examination reveals many distinctly non-traditional features, yet it is a tribute to the architect that the building conveys the strength, dignity and timelessness which many expect of the institution.

Inside, the impression of strength is reinforced by the arches springing from quite close to the floor, and the observant may notice that the thatch covers a concrete roof. The fittings are of the highest order of craftsmanship.

One theme is that of wild flowers and herbs, with forty-eight carved in local oak on the choir stalls and embroidered on an altar cloth and hymn book covers. The tapestries at either side of the altar are based on designs for a stained glass window in Salisbury Cathedral. The stained glass throughout the church has a depth and majesty of colour.

Once outside, the grounds are beautifully maintained, and over the road the neo-Jacobean lodge to Brockhampton Court doubles as a post office. Almost opposite the church and adjacent to the Brockhampton Court driveway, a vague path leads slightly to the right down a gentle valley. Go through a metal gate, the path improving, with the Court and ruined church visible on the left. At the road go right, and at the next junction right again.

Now take a track on the left and continue ahead until a junction with a path. Here go right. The path widens to become a grassy track. At the road turn left, and follow the road for about 600m.

At the Brinkley Hill car park take a track which hairpins off to the right. This descends to the river, where in places it is possible to look down on the salmon dibbling along. The river here flows smoothly past typical riverside plants, such as jumping jack, or Himalayan balsam, which flowers in late summer. The path rises through woodland, and another path plunges steeply off to the left, just before a minor road.

The riverbank is rejoined, the river often at its best - wide, shallow and shingly, with swans swimming serenely along. At Mansell's Ferry pass through a front garden, and then leave the river to walk along the base of the low bank on the right. Cross a track, but when confronted by a gate instead go through one on the right.

Climb uphill, then head left, towards a barn. Go through a gate down a short overgrown track behind the barn and follow the field boundary round to the left. Now cross the hedge or fence where practicable (no stile at the time of writing) and make for a gate to the left of a clump of trees. A stile will be espied down on the right, after which a path joins a track near a sewage works (sorry!). Go right to return to Fownhope. At the road go left.

The church, with its fourteenth-century broach spire topping a Norman spire stands on the right. It is a very long church at 36m, but its pièce de résistance is the Norman tympanum (moved to the west wall from above an external door). It is an exquisite example of the

Herefordshire School of sculpture, full of life and expression, and displaying many influences.

On the main road outside are the stocks. The author can not vouch for the milestone, which states that the distance to Hereford is $6^{1}/_{2}$ miles and 56 yards, nor that there are 22,000 shingles on the church spire. He can confirm that the village pubs are to the left, the Green Man (formerly the Naked Boy) being the best known. The liveliest day in the village calendar is the Saturday nearest 6/7 June, when the Club Walk, celebrating the Restoration of Charles II, is held.

WALK C5:
Penyard Hill

Distance:	11.5km (7m)
Map:	OS 1:25,000 Pathfinder 1065, Ross-on-Wye (East)
Start Point:	By the church at Weston under Penyard, GR 631233
Public Transport:	Hereford-Ross-Gloucester bus route
Refreshments:	Crown Inn at Howle Hill

Above the rusty sandstone of Ross stand the guardians of the Forest of Dean - the outliers of Penyard, Chase and Howle Hills. From a distance they seem to be densely wooded, but there are also upland pastures and scattered farms and hamlets. These permit long distance views, but a ruined castle and an ancient British fort are also passed on this interesting walk.

St Lawrence's church has a late Norman nave and north arcade. From the church walk uphill. At the entrance to the wood take the right-hand fork, passing through mixed woodland - ash, beech, larch and sweet chestnut predominate. Bear left then right at successive junctions before climbing out of the woods.

Walk in front of the enviably located Lawns Farm, looking over towards Dancing Green and the Hope Mansell area, probably with

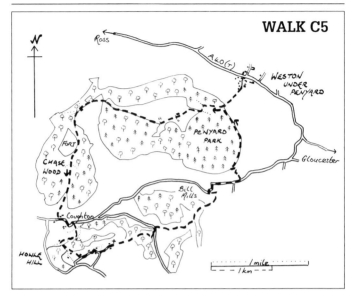

Jacob sheep in the foreground. Continue through the gate and then keep the field edge to your right. Before approaching the woodland you may be able to discern the ruins of Penyard Castle on the woodland edge to the left. Little is known of the castle's origins, although it warranted its own mint in the sixteenth century.

A stile leads to the path along the woodland edge. Go right upon joining a forestry track, which in turn bends to the right. Just before a hairpin bend, (from which there is an excellent view of the township of Ross), a short path to the left leads to a stile. From here head towards a gate in the bottom right-hand corner of the field. Shortly a stile will take you into Merrivale Wood. This is a Herefordshire Nature Trust reserve, largely oak and ash coppice, but with a range of other species including wild cherry and small-leaved lime.

The path comes out of the wood at the farm gateway. You have recently joined the Wye Valley Walk (southbound), and should now follow the appropriate waymarks. The track climbs below the ramparts of the Iron Age hill fort. It then bears away on a path, steeply downhill, and crosses a forestry track. Chase Wood and Penyard Park are detached blocks of the Forest of Dean and you are slithering into a valley cut by a former meander of the River Wye.

Upon leaving the wood look across to the right to catch a glimpse of Goodrich Castle. At the road go left, then right at the Wye Valley Walk sign. Keep along the fieldside to a stile and then pass up into the woods, to join a track, where turn right. The track curves round, but at a junction climb to the left. The track narrows to a path, but then levels out and widens after a house. You are now on Howle Hill.

The road is joined at a Methodist chapel - turn left. Ignore the lanes branching off, unless the short diversion to the Crown Inn proves irresistible. Keep on past the church. At a junction of tracks continue ahead down a narrow path - this improves as it descends through beech woods, and becomes a delightful (when dry) sunken lane.

Go left at the road, then immediately right behind Paddock Cottage. Take a stile on the right after crossing a little stream and keep to the right of Lodge Farm. After a stile bear half right - not to the head of the valley - to find a stile into the woods. Cross the path to join a slightly neglected sunken lane, uphill. After crossing another track a stile leads into a field.

Initially follow the field margin on the left, at an angle bear right

Lime flowers attract bees

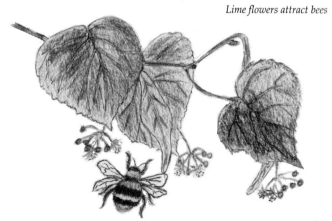

up the faint valley leading to the top of the field. There is a stile midway between two houses. Go left, then briefly down the drive, and left again down a grassy path. This descends to Bill Mills, where go right. The Mills are now the headquarters of a soft drinks firm, but there were mills here as long ago as 1418: a paper mill from 1638 to after 1821, when it became a corn mill, and the power of the Castle Brook was replaced by steam.

Pass the junction with the Hope Mansell road, then turn up the lane leading uphill to the left. Bear left, past the house, then right on the track along the woodland margin. The track can be muddy, but there are lovely views over to May Hill. Rejoin the outward route and go right to return to the village.

WALK C6:

Ross-on-Wye

Distance:	5.5km (3^1/$_2$ m)
Map:	OS 1:25,000 Pathfinder 1064, Ross-on-Wye (West)
Start Point:	Edde Cross Street car park, GR 597243
Public Transport:	Bus services to Hereford, Gloucester and Monmouth
Refreshments:	A plentitude in Ross

Ross holds a special place in the hearts of many people. At the entrance to the Wye Valley, it was the terminus for those tourists who in the early nineteenth century sought out the picturesque with fanatical zeal. Few small towns have attracted so much in the way of public benefaction from its own inhabitants. Those of John Kyrle warrant a book in themselves, but almshouses, schools, libraries, parks and water supplies were all generously given. See if Ross succeeds in winning your heart.

Turn left from the car park and walk down the hill. Pass Thrushes Nest, once the home of Sir Frederick Burrows, a railway porter who became the last governor of Bengal. Further along are

Pye's Almshouses, then turn left immediately before crossing the Rudhall Brook. Follow the roadway, then cut across a corner of the playing field to the river, here undertaking one of its famous horseshoe bends. Walk to the left, the Royal Hotel and the town's pseudo-medieval defences being clearly seen.

You are here joining the Rope Walk, rope-making being just one of the industries carried on here at one time. By the Hope and Anchor were the wharves when this was once a river port. Follow the riverside until steps lead up onto Wilton Bridge. Forty perished here in a river disaster in the reign of Elizabeth I, prior to the building of this bridge in 1599. Cross over - the sundial was placed here in the eighteenth century.

Once over the bridge take a path to the right, rather nettle-infested in high summer, and over a footbridge. Now bear left to another footbridge. On the left and somewhat masked by trees are the remains of Wilton Castle. The castle stood guard over the important Wye crossing from at least the twelfth century, but by the fifteenth century was surplus to requirements. Its owner remained neutral during the Civil War, but that did not protect it from being burnt by Parliamentarian forces. Some walls, and two towers remain, much of one tower being incorporated into an Elizabethan house, and into another in the nineteenth century.

Continue around the castle perimeter, over a stile and across a track, then through a gate, before arriving back on the road. Turn

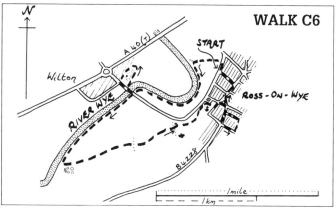

left, cross the bridge, and then immediately go down the steps on the right. Again follow the riverbank - in summer the inevitable jumping jack (Himalayan balsam) towers and dragonflies flit about. In due course the path curves inexorably towards the sewage works. Cross a track and go up the little slope to join a path heading back towards Ross along a low wooded ridge. It crosses a lane cut through the sandstone. At the next crossing path go right, then left, now joining the Wye Valley Walk. This leads into the graveyard. Detour to the left, along the cliff edge, then around to the gateway to the churchyard.

To the left is the famous view over the horseshoe bend of the Wye. The church itself is spacious indeed. The east window contains fifteenth-century stained glass figures from the Stretton Sugwas chapel of the Bishops of Hereford, and there is an alabaster tomb chest with effigies of William Rudhall, Attorney General to Henry VIII, and his wife.

From the main porch of the church a diversion to the left is recommended to have a closer look at those mock Gothic defences of 1833. Return across the frontage of the church to Church Street. Opposite are William Rudhall's almshouses, rebuilt in 1575. Turn left, then right onto High Street. Here is the bold red sandstone Market House, built in 1662 and bearing a relief of Charles II high on the east wall. Opposite is the half-timbered home of John Kyrle, who came to the town at the time the Market House was being built. He was pre-eminent amongst the town's many philanthropists. He donated the Prospect Gardens to the town, brought in a supply of fresh water, and paid for bread for the poor, to name just a few of the generous acts which led to him being immortalised by Pope as "The Man of Ross". Where are such men today?

Now go right, up Copse Cross Street. Pass Webbe's Almshouses, and at the thatched toll house turn left, down Alton Street. After the hospital a footpath leads to the left. On arriving on Old Gloucester Road the building facing you was once the Walter Scott School - not the author, but an eighteenth-century plasterer who made a fortune in London. Now go left, then right, to return to the Market House. Go downhill, along Broad Street, the main shopping street of the town.

Turn left, up Kyrle Street, passing the Button Museum, to return to the start point.

WALK C7:

Coppet Hill

Distance:	11.5km (7m)
Map:	OS 1:25,000 Outdoor Leisure 14, Wye Valley and Forest of Dean
Start Point:	Goodrich Castle car park, GR 575196
Public Transport:	Monmouth-Ross bus service halts at Goodrich School
Refreshments:	Ye Hostelrie, Goodrich
Other Information:	English Heritage booklet on Goodrich Castle

Goodrich Castle is one of those ruins that Cromwell knocked about a bit, but little imagination is required to see it as it must have been before the Civil War. From here our walk leads through Goodrich Village and then across the flank of Coppet Hill to join the River Wye. A pleasant riverside stroll follows until, under the darkening precipices of Coldwell Rocks, the main ridge of the hill is stormed, with superb views as height is gained.

It is suggested that exploration of the Castle awaits the end of the walk, so return down the track to the centre of the village. A short diversion to the right is required to find the quaint exterior of Ye Hostelrie, otherwise proceed past the school. A footpath is signed to the right, across the playing field and then diagonally left to the churchyard gate. The most notable part of the church is its fourteenth-century broach spire, which is prominent in many local views. During the Civil War the vicar was Thomas Swift (the grandfather of Dean Jonathan Swift, author of *Gulliver's Travels*), a committed Royalist. He hid the church's silver chalice and sewed 300 gold pieces into his waistcoat to take to the King at Raglan.

Continue out of the churchyard, then through another gate to the road, where go left. Where the road bends to the left a sign points along a track to the right. Obey, and at the end of the accompanying wall bear half left, downhill to a stile onto the road. Cross over and head up another track. This narrows and bends to the left, past

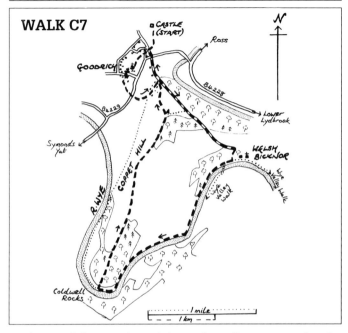

WALK C7

CASTLE (START)

Ross

GOODRICH

B4228

Lower Lydbrook

B4229

Symonds Yat

R. WYE

COPPET HILL

WELSH BICKNOR

Wye Valley Walk

Wye Valley Walk

Coldwell Rocks

1 mile
1 km

gardens, and then continues left on a lane. Contour round to the road, where go right.

There are glimpses down to the Wye, spanned by Kerne Bridge. The road climbs easily with little traffic, initially through woodland, then over more open upland. Ignore the branch to Courtfield - Henry V was supposedly nursed here in his infancy by the Countess of Salisbury. Long the home of the Vaughan family, it is now a Catholic seminary.

Take the path signed downhill to the riverside, church and youth hostel. The church requires a short detour to the left upon reaching the path at the base of the steep slope - it contains a late thirteenth-century effigy of a woman, although the church is of the mid nineteenth century. Our route follows the river to the right, now on the Wye Valley Walk. This soon crosses the Wye by a disused railway bridge, but instead we continue ahead, under the bridge.

The path becomes a little difficult for a short distance, but soon improves. Rosemary Topping rises on the opposite bank. Shortly after entering woodland a neglected monument stands to the right of the path. It is a memorial to an unfortunate youth who drowned in the river in the nineteenth century, a salutary warning of the dangers of swimming after a heavy meal in such a treacherous river. On the opposite bank are Coldwell Rocks, haunt of nesting peregrine falcons.

Look for a sign to the right, pointing the way up the steep quartz conglomerate spine of Coppet Hill. Follow the broken wall through woodland. The path levels out, and once out of the woodland there are views back to Symonds Yat. Climb towards the summit and pause to take in the views from the Black Mountains over Herefordshire and round to Penyard Hill. The ruined cottage is The Folly.

Follow the green and orange waymarks to return to the road, and go left, over the Dry Arch. To the right is Flanesford Priory - founded in 1346, only the refectory remains, and has been converted into flats. Take the track back to the Castle.

Goodric's Castle, as it was originally known, stands high above an ancient crossing place of the River Wye. Although it was in existence by the start of the twelfth century, its moment of glory came during the Civil War. Having been unoccupied for some time, the Parliamentarians installed a garrison. When they withdrew the Royalists under Sir Harry Lingen took possession. Lingen pursued a guerilla form of warfare, using Goodrich as a base to harrass the Roundheads. By late 1645 it was the only Royalist stronghold in Herefordshire. In early June 1646 Colonel John Birch set siege, using "Roaring Meg", a mortar now to be seen in Hereford. The castle was literally undermined and Lingen surrendered on 31 July.

Although the castle was "slighted" following the surrender, it seems to have escaped relatively lightly. At its heart is the small twelfth-century keep. Much of the remains date from a major rebuilding in the late thirteenth century. It has three square corner towers and a round gatehouse and chapel tower. The approach leads over a deep moat and through the barbican, an outer defence that would have to be captured before the gatehouse could be tackled.

WALK C8:

Symonds Yat

Distance:	7.5 or 8.5km (5 or 5¹/₂m)
Map:	OS 1:25,000 Outdoor Leisure 14, Wye Valley & Forest of Dean
Start Point:	Symonds Yat Rock car park, GR 563160
Public Transport:	There is a restricted bus service to Symonds Yat West (alternative start)
Refreshments:	Log Cabin at Yat Rock; The Old Ferrie Inn at Symonds Yat West

Few walks can offer sustained variety and interest, and even fewer can genuinely claim to be entirely within delectable surroundings. This walk is one of those few, with the beautiful wooded gorge of the River Wye and novelties such as an Amazonian suspension bridge, caves and a ferry. Have fun!

The car park at Yat Rock sports a small log cabin selling refreshments and postcards, from which most visitors head over the footbridge to the Rock. Perversely, we seek out a path descending from a gap in the perimeter fencing adjacent to the picnic tables, but fear not, the Rock forms part of this itinerary.

Upon meeting a track go left, still downhill. Tall, cool beech trees tower above the track. On the left a sequence of numbered boards indicates access to a range of climbs upon the crumbling limestone buttresses and pinnacles which may be glimpsed amongst the trees.

Almost reluctantly the track descends to river level, and a number of parallel paths enable closer contact with the river bank. Flotillas of canoes occupied by jovial lifejacket-clad novices are a frequent source of idle curiosity to the native wildfowl. After a while an area known as The Slaughter is passed on the left. Legends accounting for this sombre name are plentiful - battles ranging from Caratacus against the Romans, through a son of King Arthur against the Danes, Vikings, even the Civil War. Then again, it could be from "sloghtre", a Saxon word for a muddy place.

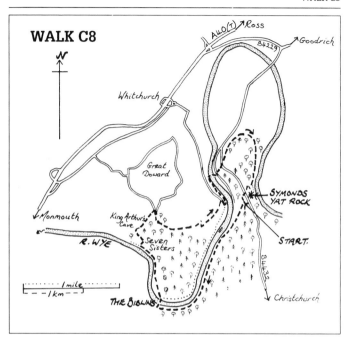

Cross the suspension bridge at The Biblins, an adventure in itself. The bridge sways as the river runs swift and deep beneath the wire mesh footway, quite exciting at a time of flood and high wind. Once again safely on dry land a choice must be made. The shorter and easier route is to turn right, along the riverside path to Symonds Yat West. On the way the Dropping Wells are passed - here water from disused iron ore workings has run over the limestone rocks and caves. The result has been stalagmites and stalactites, and deposits of tufa.

The more strenuous option goes to the left, past the former cafe at Biblins Lodge and into woodland. Keep an eye open for a waymark post indicating a path rising steeply over a scree slope on the right. The scramble leads under some of the Seven Sisters Rocks, their grandeur being somewhat masked by trees, but nevertheless they remain an impressive assemblage of oolitic limestone crags.

143

View from Yat Rock

They are undercut at their base, evidence of water action from days when the Wye had not cut so deeply into its gorge.

Waymarks lead above the rocks. On the left outcrops form lofty eyries with aerial views of the river - children take care. The path curves round to be confronted by King Arthur's Cave, which was occupied for 20,000 years during the Ice Ages. The subtle use of dynamite in 1870 revealed the bones of animals such as mammoth and cave bear which now repose in the museums of Hereford and Monmouth. It is not safe to explore too deeply.

The path continues alongside a low limestone outcrop, passing Merlin's Cave which has been much altered by iron miners, to arrive at a disused quarry. Go left, to the road where turn right then left onto a track by another old quarry. Follow the woodland margin, and where the path penetrates deeper into the wood a deep shaft is seen on the right. Just afterwards, and before a small derelict building, go right, then right again and sharply left to join a wide track descending past yet more old quarries. The buildings of Symonds Yat West come into view as you zigzag down to the road, where go right.

The road hairpins round, leading in due course to the Ferrie Boat Inn. A little passage on the right reveals the entrance to the Inn from whence the ferryman may be summoned. A small toll (50p in 1992) will see you quietly across the river. Cross the field to the road, where Wye Valley Walk waymarks lead briefly left then up through woods to cross another road and then join a forestry track.

The track curves round with glimpses of the river below. Coldwell Rocks come into sight ahead. Take a path signed to Yat Rock which zigzags steeply up to the road. Cross over and bear left to cross the track that took you outwards earlier in the day to return to the picnic area. You have now earned that visit to Yat Rock, so cross the footbridge on the left.

The views from the Rock are truly magnificent, the Wye completing a grandiose loop. It seems likely that around 2 million years ago when the sea was about 600 feet above its present level the Wye meandered just as it does now. As the sea level fell so the river cut down into the rocks below, preserving the convoluted drainage pattern of the past.

The Rock is used by the Royal Society for the Protection of Birds from late March to the end of May as a viewing platform for a pair of peregrine falcons that have taken to nesting on the crags nearby. Telescopes and wardens assist the process, and a board nearby lists other interesting birds to be seen in the woods.

Why Symonds Yat? Symonds from a former Sheriff of Herefordshire and Yat means Gate or pass - but as always there are other theories!

WALK C9:

Buckholt Wood and Welsh Newton Common

Distance:	13km (8m)
Map:	OS 1:25,000 Outdoor Leisure 14, Wye Valley and Forest of Dean
Start Point:	Lay-by on A40(T) northbound at Dixton, GR 523139
Public Transport:	Only to the centre of Monmouth, unless the driver of the Ross bus can be prevailed upon to pull into the lay-by
Refreshments:	None on route

Although close to the picturesque Wye Valley this tousled area of valley and woodland is little frequented by any but local people. Perhaps its beauty is not on open display, but those who take their time and use their powers of observation will not be disappointed. They will also be reminded that although in close proximity to the town of Monmouth, they will spend much of their day on Herefordshire soil.

At the northern extremity of the lay-by a lane leads off, hairpinning towards Newton Court. Past the Court there are open views over Monmouth before taking a lane leading off at the side of a barn, into the woods. As height is gained the views open out to include Skirrid Fawr near Abergavenny, and the mountains beyond.

The clearly waymarked track passes the ruins of Kennel Farm, shortly after which the Seven Sisters Rocks can be seen looming above the Wye Valley to the right. To their left one can pick out conifers planted at the time of the Queen's accession to form the letters "ER".

Ignore the waymarks a little further along when they suggest branching to the left. Eventually the track leads out of the woods and onto a hard surfaced lane, then into the scattered settlement of

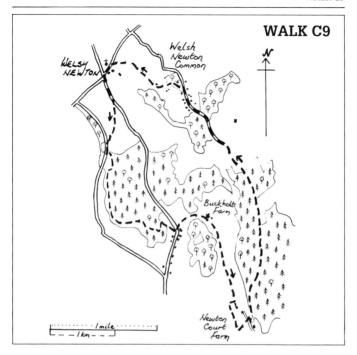

Welsh Newton Common. Turn left opposite Small Acre onto a path through woodland. At a crossing track go right and then immediately left, and soon left again. This leads to the front of Newton House. A gate on the left gives access to a field, and to the right is a gate with a bath at the side - proceed through or over either! Pause at the stile ahead where the recent tricky routefinding is rewarded by outstanding views over the Black Mountains and the Sugar Loaf.

Pass alongside a plantation, and across the first field aim for a disused farm and then steer just right of the church to arrive on a road. Turn left, and detour right to the church. Originally constructed in the thirteenth century it has some unusual features, notably the dormer window on the south side, which lights the rare stone rood screen. In the churchyard the cross is an amalgam of old and new, whilst to its left is the simple slab of the Catholic martyr John

Kemble, executed in 1679 at the age of 80.

Now walk carefully along the side of the A466 for about 200m, in the direction of Monmouth. Shortly after the milepost go through a gate on the right, rising uphill towards Broom Farm. Keep to the right of the orchard and then of an old barn, to arrive on Manson Lane. Go left, and after about 150m left again, to enter Buckholt Wood. The track curves right, and after an area of larch trees some traditionally coppiced lime trees can be seen.

When confronted by recent planting turn right, then left at the next junction. At the edge of the new planting take the path to the right, dropping part way down the slope, to join a grassy terrace path. There are views out over the Monnow Valley, before the path curves up to join the main track. Turn right, and follow the forestry track back to the A466.

Cross to the concrete track signed to Buckholt Farm, which descends into the valley of the Mally Brook amidst old-fashioned farming sights, sounds and smells (cattle, sheep, hens, barking dogs, mud...). Keep the farm buildings to your left and follow the wall. At the next field gateway bear half right, then through the gateways ahead to arrive at the gate to Newton Court Farm. Do not pass through.

Turn right and then go through a gate on the left. Follow a barely discernible path to the next gateway and head for the bridge. Once over, the path curves to a gate in the right-hand corner, where the adjoining stile should be crossed. Go left, along the field edge to pass Leasebrook bungalow. Join Golf Links Lane - keep left to rejoin the A40, from where a short but slightly un-nerving walk to the left will find the start point.

WALK C10:
Monmouth and the Kymin

Distance: 11.5km (7m)
Map: OS 1:25,000 Outdoor Leisure 14, Wye Valley and Forest of Dean

Start Point:	Free car park by the cattle market, lower Monnow Street, GR 504125
Public Transport:	Bus links to Chepstow, Ross and Newport
Refreshments:	Ample choice in Monmouth, Bush Inn at Redbrook

The contrast between an historic old town and a lofty viewing platform high above it are powerful ingredients for a stimulating walk. When mixed with a few curiosities and taken in the company of the beauty of the River Wye we have the recipe for an entertaining few hours.

Monmouth is a town which turns its back on the opportunities given by being on the banks of the rivers Wye and Monnow. Despite this it contrives to be one of the most attractive of the border towns, as a short walk will reveal.

Head out onto Monnow Street. On the left is the thirteenth-century Monnow Bridge, a unique example of a fortified bridge. Now walk up Monnow Street, simple Georgian elegance being evident in the gentle curve of the street and the façades above the

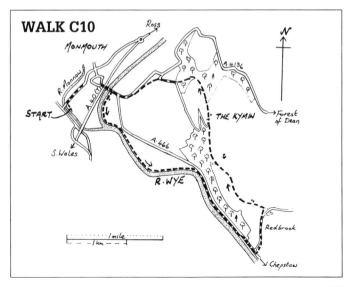

shop fronts. At the top of the hill is Agincourt Square, dominated by the Shire Hall of 1724 outside which markets add extra life and colour. Two sons of the town are commemorated by statues - that of Charles Rolls impresses far more than that of Henry V. Access to the castle ruins is almost opposite, and a little higher up the street is the museum which houses the collection of Nelson memorabilia donated by Lady Llangattock (Rolls' mother). On Priory Street the youth hostel is a former Benedictine monastery with the famous Geoffrey's Window - in fact of a later era than the historian Geoffrey of Monmouth.

From Priory Street turn down White Swan Court to Church Street, now pedestrianised, where bear left. Now go right, down St Mary's Street. Keep slightly left across the junction of St James Street and Almshouse Street.

The most dangerous part of this walk is crossing the busy A40. Over the ancient Wye Bridge descend the steps to the right. Follow the edge of the playing field, under the metal viaduct and by the remains of the stone one. The stone viaduct carried the railway from Chepstow to Monmouth, whilst the newer metal one took the line on to Ross.

The scenery here is typical of the Wye Valley, the broad river shimmering along against a background of tree clad slopes. The path clings to the upper banks, and can be slippery. The path then takes to the riverside fields before curving back to the woodland below the Redbrook road. Along here mute swans by the dozen may be seen, swimming calmly along at a discreet distance from the fishermen.

The route briefly takes to the verge of the A466 as far as the Lydney Road junction. Take the path alongside the Newland Road, gaining height and passing under the bridge which carried the Redbrook Incline down to the valley railway, after which there is no footpath. The area was an industrial centre from the early seventeenth century, with iron furnaces and copper smelting, with copper ore transported from Cornwall. Tin-plating then took over, and survived until 1961. Now these and other industries such as corn milling and brewing are just memories.

Keep an eye out for the Offa's Dyke Path waymark to take the track leading uphill on the left. Climb steadily past Duffield's Farm with views opening out over the valley. Do not be lulled into following the track too far - just before it starts to drop back into the valley a stile on the right takes us across a field below Upper Beaulieu Farm, in due course to emerge at The Kymin.

Pause for quiet contemplation. The unusual name is thought to derive from the Welsh for "a field of stone", but nowadays the eye is first drawn by the Naval Temple. Brittania proudly sits atop this building adorned with plaques bearing the names of maritime heroes of the Napoleonic Wars. The Temple was completed in 1800 and was visited two years later by Nelson in the company of Lady (and Sir William) Hamilton.

The next curiosity is the Round House, erected in 1794 for the benefit of the Gentlemen of the Kymin Club for dining purposes. The windows of the building were meticulously disposed to maximise the aesthetics of the magnificent views. The Club was also responsible for the building of the Temple, but the present condition of the buildings is due to the efforts of the National Trust - please contribute to their upkeep in the box provided.

Finally take in the panorama of Monmouth, the eye drawn over tousled countryside to the Black Mountains: a place to linger!

Descent is simple, as Offa's Dyke waymarks are present at every turn. Pass through woodland and pasture to the A4136, and thence over the Wye Bridge and along Almshouse, Glendower and Monnow Streets to return to the car park.

WALK C11:
Redbrook and Newland

Distance:	9km (5$^{1}/_{2}$m)
Map:	OS 1:25,000 Outdoor Leisure 14, Wye Valley and Forest of Dean
Start Point:	Lay-by at junction of A466 and B4231 at Redbrook, GR 535102
Public Transport:	Chepstow to Monmouth bus route
Refreshments:	Bush Inn and Little Chef at Redbrook, The Ostrich at Newland

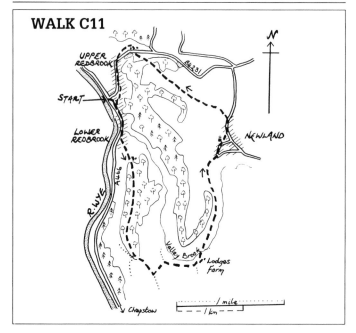

WALK C11

Redbrook sits by the River Wye, a former industrial centre now on the restless Monmouth to Chepstow road. From here the walk climbs by way of the Offa's Dyke Path, before descending to a valley which was once home to the Wye. On the brink of this valley is the village of Newland, with its large and fascinating church, from whence it is an easy return walk across upland fields.

Walk from the lay-by along the main road in the direction of Tintern and Chepstow. Look for the Offa's Dyke Path waymark after a service station on the left. The path climbs steeply, over a road and towards Highbury Farm, then keep to the right of the farm to enter Highbury Wood National Nature Reserve. The sign at the entrance explains that this is an ancient semi-natural example of Wye Valley broadleaved woodland.

The path is faithful to Offa's Dyke until it crosses Coxbury Lane, which we follow to the left. To the right are views over to the Wye

Valley, and then the valley to the left also becomes visible. Take a stile on the left, head straight down the side of the field and over another stile. Now go right, along the valley bottom. You are here walking in a long-abandoned meander of the River Wye, which once took a long detour from Redbrook to Newland and thence back to what is now the main valley. The detour is 8.5km, where 0.5km now suffices.

At Lodges Farm keep below the buildings and close to the Valley Brook, going through a metal gate and over some lowered fences to rejoin the farm track. Go left and follow this gentle climb towards Newland. Join a lane and bear right at an idiosyncratic bungalow with carved bargeboards, then climb steeply left.

At the top of the hill is the church of All Saints, "The Cathedral of the Forest". The late fourteenth-century tower with its five pinnacles initially draws the eye, but most of the interest lies inside. There are effigies of Sir John Joce and his wife from the mid-fourteenth century, his head resting on a helm bearing the head of a Saracen. Slightly later, are two effigies of priests, but the two most intriguing images are of a forester and the Miner's Brass. The first, to be found in the south aisle, is an incised slab depicting a seventeenth-century bowman, complete with horn and dagger. By way of contrast nearby rests the effigy of Jenkin Wyrall, the Forester of Fee, who died in 1457.

The Miner's Brass is to be found in the south chapel. It appears that a fifteenth-century brass to Robert Gryndour was altered for Sir Christopher Baynham a century later. At this time was added a helmet with a crest showing a miner with a hod and pick, clasping a candle holder in his mouth.

From this church came powerful men, such as Walter Giffard who was rector here in 1247. He rose to become Chancellor of England and Archbishop of York. The church now stands in a large close, along the south side of which are the almshouses founded in 1615 by William Jones, a citizen and haberdasher of London. To the east is the Ostrich Inn, reputed to be haunted. We head north, along the village street, until a sign on the left, pointing to Upper Redbrook, is to be obeyed.

Bear half right to an angle in the field - peek through the hedge to see the Great Oak of Newland, now a sorry stump. The path is well waymarked as it switches from one side of the hedge to the other and back again. It passes above Swanpool Wood, at a safe distance from the Pool, with its fearsome ghostly inhabitants - a black dog, a baby crying from afar, and "a tall woman in white, draped with dripping weed and a moaning child in arms rising from the water".

Our path descends uneventfully through Furnace Wood to the road. Bear slightly right to cross to another path. Don't be tempted to continue along the Offa's Dyke Path - turn left alongside a cottage to return to the road. Turn left just before the old incline bridge to keep away from the road. Rejoin the A466 and go right to find the start point again.

WALK C12:

Tintern Abbey and the Devil's Pulpit

Distance: 7km (4¹/₂m)
Map: OS 1:25,000 Outdoor Leisure 14, Wye Valley
                       and Forest of Dean
Start Point: Tintern Abbey car park, GR 532001
Public Transport: On Chepstow to Monmouth bus route
Refreshments: Pubs and cafes in Tintern
Further Information: Cadw booklet on Tintern Abbey

Each year many thousands of people visit Tintern Abbey, sited conspicuously in the valley of the lower Wye. Most stroll around the Abbey buildings, and some venture into the craft shops in the village. Sadly, to gain a real impression of the Abbey in its surroundings one must leave behind the busy A466, the car parks and the milling crowds. From a little distance one can gain some appreciation of this jewel in its setting. Perspective of distance helps in appreciating the perspective of time.

From the car park leave the crowds behind and head for the start of the Tintern Trail. This leads upstream along the riverbank then inland to the main road. Turn right, then right again, over the old

WALK C12

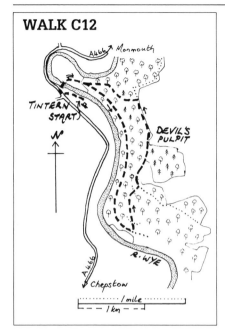

bridge which once carried a branch of the Wye Valley line over the river. Now head downstream, with glimpses of the Abbey through the trees.

Ignore a sign to the Devil's Pulpit and trek along the disused railway line. The blocked tunnel entrance on the left is an obvious relic of the railway age - others lie shrouded by vegetation, waiting to be spotted by the assiduous. Some may be more interested in wild flowers, such as viper's bugloss, and trees including beech, lime and hazel.

A Wye Valley Countryside Service waymark points to the left, and should be obeyed. The route then curves left, across a track, climbing all the time and liberally waymarked. Left onto another track, then steeply right before the climbing eases and on the left is our first viewing point. This is Plumweir Cliff, with Tintern in the distance below.

Continuing along the valley rim, you are now on a stretch of the Offa's Dyke Path. There are other viewing points, one with a memorial seat, before the rocky outcrop of the Devil's Pulpit is reached. From here the Devil is alleged either to have preached or ranted and raved at the holy brethren below.

Continue along the path, here running in the ditch of Offa's Dyke, with the bank, still of impressive size, on the right. A sign for Tintern indicates the onset of the descent. Some care in routefinding is necessary, despite the waymarks, and at one point a pause is

Tintern Abbey

justified, by a stone wall where a cliff falls sheer to the river. The path joins our outward route (turn right, go over the bridge and back to the Abbey).

Now the Abbey can be explored. It was founded by the Cistercians in 1131, although the ruins are mainly of the thirteenth century. The cruciform church is still a remarkable relic, with impressive decorated tracery to the west window and the fifteenth-century cloisters to the north. Contrasting with this magnificence are features such as the warming room, the sole source of warmth for the monks. Although founded as an austere order, as a reaction against the decadence of others, the Cistercians themselves left their early ideals behind, easing Henry VIII's task at the Dissolution.

Geologists will delight in the variety of stone used, from local Devonian sandstone, Dundry oolite, purple sandstone and pink quartz conglomerate, which add subtle variation to the harmony of the building. Remains of many of the buildings on the site are vestigial, but sufficient remains to be able to interpret something of the scale of development on this site, and of monastic life. Most visitors will leave imbued with a sense of the great belief which drove men to build such an edifice in what was then little more than a wilderness, but no one should forget that this later became an industrial centre. Wire, iron and brass were all produced hereabouts - wiredrawing began in 1566, being much in demand for carding wool - and a plaque proclaims (perhaps wrongly), that brass was first made here.

Much time can be spent pottering around the site, although the excellent Cadw booklet is required to gain full benefit, hence the reason for doing the walk first...

WALK C13:
The Narth

Distance:	5km (3m)
Map:	OS 1:25,000 Outdoor Leisure 14, Wye Valley and Forest of Dean
Start Point:	Manor Wood car park, GR 529059
Public Transport:	Some Monmouth to Chepstow bus services run via The Narth
Refreshments:	The Trekkers Inn at The Narth

A short stretch of the Wye Valley Walk, woodland on the valley sides and some fine views are the main elements of this short walk.

Return to the road from the car park and turn left. The road curves right, a telephone kiosk being passed on your right at a crossroads. The Wye Valley Walk rises up the hillside to join the road near the Duke of Beaufort's Lodge.

Woodland is entered, and after some marshy ground on the right some trees have been cleared on the left to provide a view over the Wye towards Bigsweir. At this point turn right, off the main track. Cross a forestry track to enter a shady path. At the end go right, to pass through the scattered community of Maryland.

Cross the road and head off down another forestry track. Take the first turning to the right, and ignore the many confusing minor paths that branch off, unless you wish to have a closer look at some

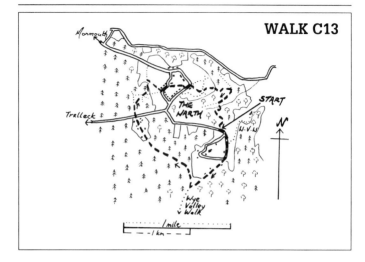

WALK C13

of the impressive piles of cast-off needles accumulated by the industrious wood ant communities.

Leave the wood by a stile at the side of a gate, with views now over the Whitebrook Valley. The power of the brook served wire works from 1606 to around 1720, and later corn mills until the end of the nineteenth century. On the right a moveable timber barrier leads into a field, at the end of which bear left down an overgrown path to the road. Go left.

Where the road bears left we continue ahead along a lane. At a fork go right to arrive at another road, where turn left. The former workers' cottages have almost all been modernised out of recognition, as The Narth has become a particularly salubrious community.

Turn right down a No Through Road after the Trekkers Inn. Follow this road downhill, ignoring turnings off, to arrive at what appears to be a dead end, with a sign for Coney's Oak Cottage. In fact the path initially runs alongside and to the right of the driveway, passing close to the cottage, and then down a steep flight of steps to a forestry track. Go right, and in a short distance is a seat at a viewpoint over a side valley and the Wye.

Further on look for a signboard to your right, opposite which a path descends to a footbridge. Once over and through a marshy area, climb to the right. Just as the ascent eases turn to the left, to climb steadily through beech woods and return to the car park.

WALK C14:
Brockweir to Bigsweir

Distance:	14km (8¹/₂m)
Map:	OS 1:25,000 Outdoor Leisure 14, Wye Valley and Forest of Dean
Start Point:	Tintern Station, GR 536006
Public Transport:	Chepstow to Monmouth bus service
Refreshments:	Tintern Station, pubs in Brockweir and St Briavels

The title may indicate a gentle riverside stroll on the banks of the Wye. So it is - on the return. First there is a climb onto the plateau, through countryside which in high season displays a wealth of wild flowers, to the village of St Briavels. Here the castle was the administrative hub of the Forest of Dean. Back through pleasant woodland and along the ever-lovely Wye, this is a walk of real quality.

The original Victorian station on the former Wye Valley line has been rescued from dereliction to serve as a visitor centre, complete with information office and cafe. From here head north, passing the signal box on your right, along the old railway track. Climb the steps to Brockweir bridge and cross the river. The bridge was built in 1904, signalling the end of the ferry that once operated here. The river can rise 3 metres or more during the spring tides which arise about twice each month.

Brockweir itself was once second only to Chepstow as a Wye port, at one time harbouring sixteen pubs. Turn right at the Brockweir Country Inn. It is worth taking a brief diversion to the Moravian church, down the passageway to the right. Here are the graves of Ebenezer Henderson Smith, editor of *The Boys Own Paper,* and his

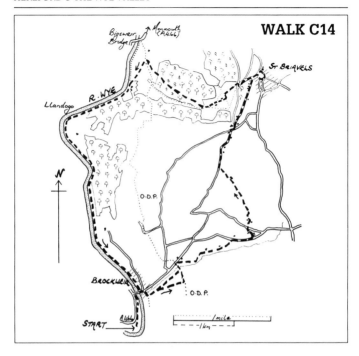

wife, Flora Klickman, editor of the feminine equivalent and author of the *Flower Patch Stories.*

Return up the passageway and turn right, then follow the Offa's Dyke Path waymarks left, gates leading by the Horses and Ponies Rescue Association stables and adjoining paddocks. After the fourth gate a sign points downhill to the left across a little wooded valley. Turn right on a path just before the road to join a lane. Where this turns left continue ahead on a path, beset by hazel, holly, blackthorn, hawthorn and lime. Go right on joining a shady and narrow country lane.

At the next road junction turn left, then cross another road. Go left on a path, in front of Hartlands. This path bends left and right, now with views over the Wye Valley. Along here are brambles and foxgloves, redcurrants and kidney vetch, also yarrow, to name but a few. The path becomes a lane, and then a road, where go right.

This is Sandy Lane, which joins another road, where go briefly right and then left by the post box. Keep to the upper road, which follows the edge of one of those abandoned meander valleys of the Wye, to enter St Briavels. Upon arriving at a road junction go up a path on the right. This brings you to the heart of the village. Now follow the perimeter of the castle to the right, leading round to the gatehouse.

The castle was built in 1131 by Milo Fitzwater, Earl of Hereford, and was the administrative headquarter for the Forest of Dean. Guests included King John - nowadays they are youth hostellers. At least they are not accommodated in the oubliette, a dungeon accessed only by a trapdoor in the ceiling.

Although the village is named after the fifth-century hermit Brigomaglos, the church across the road is dedicated to St Mary. The tower and much of the chancel is of the nineteenth century, but there are fragments dating back to the twelfth century. The font is Norman, and there is a carved stone coffin lid of about 1300 in the south transept. More interesting than the building itself is the bread and cheese ceremony, celebrated after Evensong on Whit Sunday. It supposedly originated when Milo Fitzwater and his wife won the right for the villagers to collect wood nearby, and in gratitude the parishioners gave bread and cheese to the poor. At one stage it was abandoned because it was becoming too unruly.

On leaving the churchyard gate turn right, ignore the first road to the right, and continue downhill (signed to Lower Meend). Another road joins from the right, then go round a very sharp right-hand bend and immediately take the path (signed) to the left. This takes you down some steps by a house (waymarked) and so to a lane. Now turn left, then right, passing Cherry Tree Farm on the right and then Woodcroft on the left.

Where the lane bends sharply left take a path to the right. This path forks: choose the right hand branch, through lovely beechwoods, with clumps of cow wheat underfoot during the summer. The path crosses Offa's Dyke in its way downhill.

On leaving the wood keep somewhat to the right, passing a stunted sweet chestnut tree. Now proceed along the avenue (predominantly of oaks) to the left. This passes Bigsweir House and joins the low level alternative of the Offa's Dyke Path, staying close to the river. On the opposite bank the village of Llandogo is soon passed, the limit of tidal navigation in former days. Another kilometre sees Coed Ithel weir. On the opposite side of the river was a sixteenth-century blast furnace. Although its work ended around 1700, part still remains.

The remainder of the walk is straightforward, returning to Brockweir. In front of Quay House is the screw and shaft of the last boat to sail to Brockweir - the Belle Marie, in 1914 (or so it is said). Cross the bridge and go over the stile on the left to return to Tintern Station.

Foxglove

WALK C15:
Trelleck Curiosities

Distance:	2km (1¹/₂m)
Map:	OS 1:25,000 Outdoor Leisure 14, Wye Valley and Forest of Dean (not essential)
Start Point:	Car park in Trelleck, GR 501453
Public Transport:	Chepstow to Monmouth bus route
Refreshments:	Village Green and Lion Inns

Trelleck is an odd sort of place - an ordinary village bisected by a busy road, but with more than its fair share of interesting features - the church, a motte, standing stones and a holy well. There is history here, and more than a little mystery too.

From the car park by the chapel turn right, along the village street (once part of Watling Street West), and cross to the churchyard. The church of St Nicholas has a curious sundial of 1689, and a much

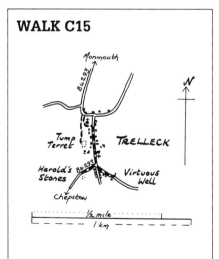

restored preaching cross of the eighth or ninth century. It has three fonts - one Saxon, one Norman and one Early English. When the pulpit was installed in 1640 it was a three-decker.

On leaving the church head for the gate in the north-western corner of the church-yard, and then take the path signed immediately to the left. This leads to Tump Terret, a substantial motte of

163

The Virtuous Well

137m (450ft) diameter.

Return down the path, across the churchyard, and again down the village street. Continue to the right on the B4293, to see on the left Harold's Stones, or Devil's Arrows. These three pudding stone (pebbly sandstone) objects were used for a Bronze Age long barrow. They gave the village it's name - Trelleck means the three stones.

Now return down the road and continue over the crossroads on the Tintern road. Soon seen on the left is the sign for the Virtuous Well, restored in 1951. The legend is that if you throw a stone in and bubbles rise, your wish will be granted. It does not say when.

Back again down the road and right is the start point. Trelleck was once a prosperous little town, but fell foul of the Duke of Norfolk amidst suspicions of deer poaching. He razed the little town to the ground in 1291. The fourteenth-century Black Death and the deprivations caused by Owain Glendwr ensured that it never recovered.

WALK C16:
Wintour's Leap

Distance:	10km (6¹/₂m)
Map:	OS 1:25,000 Outdoor Leisure 14, Wye Valley and Forest of Dean
Start Point:	Welsh Street car park, Chepstow, GR 533939
Public Transport:	Chepstow has main line rail and bus connections with Gloucester and South Wales
Refreshments:	Ample choice in Chepstow; pub in St Arvans
Further Information:	Cadw booklet on Chepstow Castle

Chepstow is an attractive and interesting border town at the confluence of the Wye and the Severn. At its heart is its castle, a textbook in stone of this instrument of domination and control. The walk progresses from here past limestone cliffs close by the river, with one section where care and agility are required, before climbing onto the plateau, to be rewarded by sweeping views over the Severn estuary. This walk is not advisable when the Wye is in flood.

The car park is protected by the thirteenth-century Port Wall, and from its fringe can be gained an early appreciation of the strategic position and design of the castle. A pedestrian exit leads into Beaufort Square, at the lower end of which St Mary Street has been pedestrianised with an almost continental result.

Bear left onto Church Street and then right to Bridge Street - here at the top are the Powys almshouses of 1716, and lower down is the castle entrance. William Fitz Osbern started building here soon after he was created Earl of Hereford immediately after the Conquest. The hall-keep that resulted is the "earliest datable secular stone building in Britain". The castle was subject to regular strengthening in line with contemporary military architecture until about 1300, by which time the Welsh had largely been subjugated.

Prominent from the path to the front is the outer gatehouse, with Marten's Tower (named after the regicide imprisoned here at the

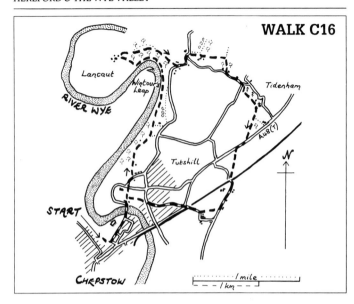

Restoration) easily distinguished by the sculpted stone figures on the battlements. A detailed inspection of the interior should not be missed, but is perhaps better undertaken at the end of the walk.

Continuing downhill we cross Rennie's bridge of 1816, above the Wye, here heavily laden with sediment. On the cliff opposite a painted Union Jack identifies Gloucester Hole, an enlarged natural cave, possibly used to store gunpowder for the castle at one stage, and certainly used for explosives by Brunel when constructing his wrought iron railway bridge. Once over the bridge take the footway directly ahead to ascend the hillside. Cross the A48 to a cycleway, then take the stile on the left marked by an Offa's Dyke Footpath sign. This field path passes the ruins of a sixteenth-century beacon tower before turning right, and then left down a passage.

Don't gaze too long at the impressive house opposite or you will miss the stile on the left. Once across the field pass under a little footbridge to enter the Lancaut Nature Reserve. The path descends through woodland with quarries to the right - it is worth detouring slightly to appreciate the height and extent of these cliffs. These quarries in the Drybrook sandstone provided the stone for Avonmouth Docks. As the path descends to the river it becomes more Himalayan in character, with vigorous vegetation such as buddleia and a boulder field to be traversed.

We join the river at its longest straight stretch (1km), but soon follow it round, and have the opportunity to look back at the 60m limestone cliffs of Wintour's Leap. Supposedly Sir John Wintour, on horseback, was attempting to escape his Parliamentarian pursuers during the Civil War. He leaped over the cliff and survived to swim the Wye to safety. The path leads away from the river at the ruined church of St James which marks the site of an abandoned settlement. Our path bears to the left of a large oak tree to join a track. Go right.

Immediately after a cattle grid take a path through woods to the right, passing limekilns to rejoin the road - right again. On the left is the site of an Iron Age fort, and soon part of Offa's Dyke can be discerned. Most eyes will be drawn in the direction of the Severn Estuary, with the bridge prominent.

At the B4228 go left (no pavement). In quick succession on the right are Netherhope Lane, the entrance to Ashberry House and the stile to be taken, to run alongside the tall garden wall of the House. Over a track, through a gate, and then follow the fieldside on the left. Another gate and then go right at a stile on the left, to meet the road.

Now go left, over the old Wye Valley railway line, tracks still intact and the tunnel portal below. Go over a stile in the angle of a road junction to enter woodland, and then bear left, having read the quarry warning notice. At the next stile go right, past ruined buildings and high walls. At another path junction go right unless wishing to detour briefly to inspect Tidenham church. The tower was once used as a beacon for shipping in the estuary.

At the bottom of the slope ignore the footpath sign pointing left and continue ahead, alongside the quarry. At the top of the slope the immense depth and extent of this gouge into the Lower Dolomite is manifest. Now descend the steps and go right.

Opposite the quarry entrance is a gate - go through and follow the field edge, alongside the railway. Go left at the road, over the main rail line. After about 300m a stile will be found on the right - go over this and one more stile and a gate on the left lead to a minor road, where go right.

Cross the A48 (with extreme care) and walk through suburban Tutshill. Cross the B4228 to a footway, and turn left where it rejoins the outward route. On recrossing the bridge the natural defences of the castle, perched on the very edge of the limestone cliff, are even more evident.

WALK C17:
Wynd Cliff

Distance:	12km (7¹/₂m)
Map:	OS 1:25,000 Outdoor Leisure 14, Wye Valley and Forest of Dean
Start Point:	Welsh Street car park, Chepstow, GR 533939
Public Transport:	Chepstow is well served by rail and bus services
Refreshments:	Ample choice in Chepstow, also Piercefield Hotel, St Arvans

This walk traverses the countryside between Chepstow and St Arvans, before visiting the Eagle's Nest, a truly spectacular viewpoint. The return is along part of the Wye Valley Walk, high above the river itself and with outstanding views from attractive sylvan surroundings.

Return to Welsh Street and go left, then right. Now turn right then left, to join Mounton Road. This climbs steadily through suburban Chepstow, crossing the A466, and then passing the hospital. The road descends to the hamlet of Bayfield.

The road bends right at a junction, and on the next left-hand bend are two stiles in close proximity - take the one to the right of the farm gate, at the side of the house, and follow the field edge down the hill. Go over another stile and then take a gate into the woods on the right. The little path soon joins a track, where go right. Take a track (possibly muddy) that branches off to the left - follow this as it bends left. At a concrete Water marker post go up the slope on the right.

WALK C17

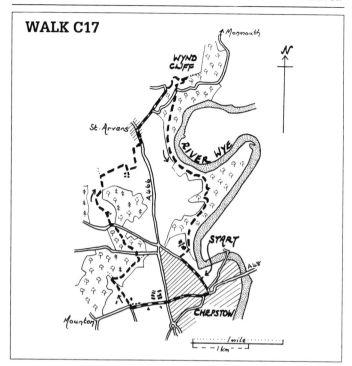

Cross the road to enter Cockshoot Wood. Upon leaving the wood go slightly left and cross the road to a stile adjacent to the imposing entrance of Rossfield. Follow the field margin past the farm. When the hedge expires angle right to the corner of Fryth Wood.

Peek inside the entrance to the wood to see one of the footpath maps installed by St Arvans Community, a pleasing sight. With your back to the wood entrance walk along the side of the hay meadow. Over a stile, then go right, over another stile and a fence to a gate. Follow the field edge right, left and left again to another gate by the sewage works. Go through to the road and turn left.

Pass through the village of St Arvans and continue along the main road. At the junction to Wynd Cliff walk up the minor road.

At the top is a car park, with the waymarked route climbing to the Eagle's Nest. Take this path, initially passing the sign for the 365 steps before dropping down to the Eagle's Nest.

The railed viewpoint hangs high above the valley side, looking over the loops of the Wye curling round towards Chepstow, and over the Severn as far as the Cotswolds. The initial impact should be tempered by a lengthy study of the panorama spread out before you - allegedly as far as Devon on a really clear day.

Retrace your route and then turn left, down the 365 steps. Nothing further removed from a domestic staircase can be envisaged. Constructed in 1828/9 on the instructions of the Duke of Beaufort (like the Eagle's Nest), these are giant steps, rugged, haphazard, and at one point spanning a small ravine. The atmospheric location is enhanced by moss covered rocks and gloomy yew trees. This is just the spot to set a Gothik horror story.

Cross the A466 and follow the waymarks for the Wye Valley Walk, seemingly suspended above the river, with glimpses across to the Lancaut peninsula. There are still further intrigues, such as a tunnel and a cave, as Chepstow is approached. The Walk passes through the grounds of Piercefield House (now derelict), which were landscaped in the romantic style during the eighteenth century by Valentine Morris. Some of the grottoes and other delights still remain.

Re-enter Chepstow by the side of the Leisure Centre and turn left to return to the start.

THE FOREST OF DEAN

INTRODUCTION

The Forest is an intriguing place, far more than a vast expanse of trees. For long it was a secretive and introspective world. Bounded on three sides by the rivers Severn and Wye, this is a rugged upland area, dissected by steep-sided valleys and cloughs. Once a Royal Forest, the hunting preserve of a privileged few, it has a parallel industrial history which shaped its present character.

Iron-mining, coal-mining and quarrying scarred the landscape, and until the middle years of this century large parts were disfigured by these activities. Strangely, the economic exploitation of these natural resources (often coupled with excessive timber extraction) declined just as the mass recreational potential of the Forest itself began to be widely recognised.

Today, the vast spoil heaps have been removed or landscaped, and tree planting and natural revegetation have softened these once lurid scars. The Forestry Commission has developed car parks, picnic areas and waymarked routes for walkers, cyclists and horse riders. Fortunately, large numbers of visitors can be concealed within the quietude of this leafy expanse.

The underlying landscape, streams and ponds, industrial relics, wildlife and sheer variety of tree planting ensure that the Forest is not simply a vast, silent and monotonous commercial plantation. It is a fascinating place to be, with surprising glimpses from higher ground out to the surrounding countryside and the Severn Estuary.

Regrettably, most of the larger towns and villages, such as Cinderford and Mitcheldean, lack any vestige of charm, but others, such as Staunton, Clearwell and Newland, are both attractive and interesting.

One word of warning. The network of paths and tracks can be extremely confusing, even with the aid of maps and liberal waymarking, so take care with routefinding. A compass can be more helpful here than on the wild hills!

Geology, Iron- and Coal-mining

The Forest is founded on a syncline - a basin-shaped fold in the underlying rocks. The dip is steeper to the east, so the outcrops are narrower there. The succession starts with the Lower Devonian (Brownstones), followed by the Upper Devonian of quartz conglomerate and Tintern sandstone. The conglomerate (or puddingstone) is frequently met on the walks in this book, as it forms a girdle around the Forest, often creating an escarpment as at The Buckstone on Walk D8.

Next are the Carboniferous rocks - first the white to pinkish-grey limestone, then the pink to yellow Drybrook sandstone. Finally come the grey sandstones of the Pennant Series of the Upper Coal Measures, resting in the centre of the basin. The Forest is an upland of around 168m (550ft) above sea level in the central region, with a high ridge of about 244m (800ft) in the north and 183-244m (600-800ft) on the flanks of the Wye.

Stone has been quarried here for centuries. By 1858 there were no less than 320 quarries in the Forest, mostly in the Pennant sandstone. Even quite recently local stone has been taken as far afield as the University College of Wales in Aberystwyth, University College London, and to Sheffield and Belfast. Bixslade quarry is visited on Walk D6, but most quarrying is now on the fringes of the Forest itself. The Lower Dolomite is extracted at Drybrook (Walk D10), Staunton, Newland and Tidenham.

The Pennant sandstones are interspersed with coal seams, especially the Coleford High Delph. These seams were worked by the Romans, and the industry was well under way by 1300. The miners of the area were granted special privileges, set out in the Book of Dennis, reputedly for their work as sappers for Edward I at the siege of Berwick. "Freeminers" must be born of a Free father, within the Hundred of St Briavels (approximating to the Forest), be over twenty-one years of age and have worked in a coal mine for at least a year and a day Freeminers are granted rights - known as "gales" - to mine at particular locations. Gales, mining laws and the determination of disputes are administered by the Deputy Gaveller, who presides over the Court of Mine Law at Coleford. He also collects the Queen's dues, or taxes, as he has always done.

By 1880 the small-scale activities of the freeminer had been overshadowed by the large collieries - there were sixty-three in operation by this time. Their most attractive features were often their names, such as Work or Hang, Strip and At It, Speculation and New Fancy. Amalgamation followed Edwardian mining acts, resulting in just six large collieries remaining. The industry declined after the Second World War - not surprisingly in some cases - Cannop Colliery had to remove 100 tons of water for every ton of coal produced. The last big pit closed in 1965.

Beneath the Carboniferous limestone are large iron ore deposits. It is believed that during the Permian period (280-225 million years BP) the arid landscape was eroded and iron-rich solutions permeated downwards, particularly into the open-textured Crease limestone.

Charcoal for smelting was in ample supply, despite charcoal burning being banned in 1270 due to the extent of timber depletion. This did not prevent there being over 2,000 hearths recorded in 1282.

The Romans had an iron industry under way by the 2nd century AD. The early smelting methods were understandably inefficient, so the introduction of the charcoal blast furnace in the sixteenth century resulted in the original waste heaps being re-smelted. By 1826 there were coke-fired furnaces at Cinderford and Parkend - the latter having the blast powered by a 15.5m (51ft) waterwheel. The storage ponds used to drive the waterwheel are at Cannop, and are visited on Walks D5 and D6. Flaxley (Walk D2) was another centre for the forgemasters.

The major problem with the iron reserves was that the ores were faulted, rendering mining increasingly difficult. Smelting had ceased by the end of the nineteenth century, and mining by World War 2. Many of the open workings, known as Scowles, can still be seen, notably around Clearwell (Walk D7).

Railways

The Forest is traversed by a complex network of former railways and tramways, built to serve the quarries and mines. The earliest date from 1810, although steam power did not arrive until 1864. By the time the Great Western Railway completed the Severn Tunnel in 1886 the railway business was already in decline. The only remnant is a 7km (4^{1}/2m) stretch from Lydney Junction to Parkend, under the protection of the Forest of Dean Railway Preservation Society. Steam engines run from the Norchard Steam Centre over the southern part of this section. Otherwise the trackbeds now form easily graded and well-drained footpaths through the Forest.

Forestry and Natural History

Recognised for its hunting potential by Canute, the area was designated a Royal Forest by William the Conqueror. The full extent was 48,560ha (120,000 acres), of which only around one quarter is now woodland. The headquarters of the Forest administration were at St Briavels castle (walk C14), where the Warden enforced the laws which protected the game and its habitat.

Penalties of death or maiming for harming the Forest or game were later commuted to fines as hunting diminished in importance. Later still the fines became regarded as no more than taxes, or rent.

The use of Forest timber for charcoal for iron-smelting has previously been mentioned. It also proved to be a valuable resource for ship-building - indeed the Spanish Armada was reputedly tasked to destroy the Forest, such was its fame.

Efforts were made during the Commonwealth period to protect the depleting timber resources. A Reafforestation Act followed in 1668. The Forest was divided into six "walks", each with a house, known as a lodge, to house the Forest official responsible for that walk. One, Danby Lodge, is visited on walk D4. 4,450ha (11,000 acres) were to be enclosed as nurseries for naval shipbuilding timber, within which area commoners rights were removed. This attempt to enforce stricter control led to a reaction and ensuing rioting. In the event only a fraction of the proposed planting resulted.

The Speech House (Walk D9) was built in 1682 to house the Verderers Court following further attempts to revitalise planting and management- it is now a Trust House Hotel. Decline set in once more, with the Napoleonic Wars spurring exploitation. More reorganisation, enclosures, and lodges (of a simpler nature) for the keepers and foresters reflected another attempt to impose order. Highmeadow Woods, an outlier of the main Forest, was purchased by the Crown in 1817. Natural setbacks included a plague of mice and voles in 1813, which destroyed 200,000 trees, 100,000 vermin being trapped.

After World War 2 the planting of swifter growing conifers expanded and oak tended to be replaced by beech. Of 12,550ha (31,000 acres) no less than 10,930ha (27,000 acres) are owned by the Forestry Commission. It operates a policy of ensuring that about half the woodland is broadleaved. In 1938 this was the nation's first Forest Park, laying the foundation for the integration of economic forestry with nature conservation and recreational provision that now characterises the area. 70,000 tonnes of timber are produced from the Forest each year.

The oak woodlands of the Cannop Valley are particularly significant, dating back to the replanting ordered by Admiral Lord Nelson, Conifers include Douglas fir and Norway spruce, whilst conspicuous in the pine plantations (largely Corsican and Scots pines) are the heaps of needles accumulated by wood ants.

Grasshoppers can be heard cheeping during the summer. In June and July the lakes and ponds, fringed by willow, alder and silver birch, harbour the emperor dragonfly. Other dragonflies and damselflies are seen later in the summer. One of the most spectacular species is the beautiful demoiselle, which frequents fast-flowing streams. It has an iridescent green body and blue/black wings. The easiest method of distinguishing between dragonflies and damselflies is that the former close their wings upon landing whilst the latter rest with their wings spread.

White Admiral

Peacock butterfly

In May the black-spotted and pearl-bordered fritillary butterflies flit around, to be followed later by the silver-washed fritillary and the white admiral. At the Nagshead reserve of the Royal Society for the Protection of Birds no less than thirty-five species of butterfly have been recorded.

One would expect this vast expanse of forest to be rich in birdlife, and so it is. Throughout the year woodpeckers, nuthatches, hawfinches and treecreepers are resident. Migrants arriving March onwards include chiffchaffs, blackcaps, willow warblers, the striking pied flycatcher, wood warblers and redstarts. Winter sees those typical roving bands of blue, great, long-tailed and other tits, perhaps joined by a lesser spotted woodpecker. Flocks of redwings, fieldfares, siskins and redpolls also scavenge the trees. Buzzards are often seen overhead and sometimes sparrowhawks and ravens likewise. The ponds attract moorhen, mallard and little grebe with visiting herons.

Two herds of fallow deer roam the Forest, and glimpses can sometimes be snatched. They, and the long-vanished wild boar, were the reason for the area originally being designated a Royal Forest. Red and roe deer were also present at that time, but hunting and poaching depleted their stocks and rendered them locally extinct. Indeed, 1850 saw a Deer Removal Act, to reduce damage to timber production and to eliminate poaching. A few fallow deer struggled on in Highmeadow Woods, where their numbers built up to their current levels of about 150. A smaller herd roams in the woods near the Speech House.

Foxes and badgers are the other larger wild mammals present, with grey squirrels scampering restlessly around. Sheep are seen grazing in the woods, on the roadside verges and even in the towns.

176

Originally they were not permitted in the Forest, but were introduced with the breakdown of the Forest laws. Their numbers are now regulated by an agreement between the Forestry Commission and the Commoners. Those who own the sheep are known as "ship badgers".

Fly Agaric (see p185)

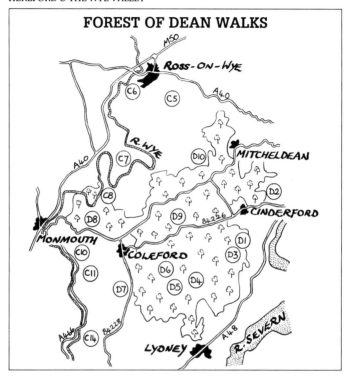

FOREST OF DEAN WALKS

LIST OF WALKS

D1:	BLAIZE BAILEY	10.5km	6½m
D2:	FLAXLEY	7.0km	4½m
D3:	SOUDLEY	4.0km	2½m
D4:	STAPLE EDGE AND MALLARDS PIKE	8.5km	5½m
D5:	NEW FANCY TO NAGSHEAD	9.0km	5½m
D6:	CANNOP AND BIXSLADE	11.0km	7m
D7:	CASTLES AND CAVES	5.0km	3m
D8:	ROCKS AND STONES	5.5km	3½m
D9:	SPEECH HOUSE & THE SCULPTURE TRAIL	6.5km	4m
D10:	RUARDEAN	9.0km	5½m

WALK D1:
Blaize Bailey

Distance:	10.5km (6$^{1}/_{2}$m)
Map:	OS 1:25,000 Outdoor Leisure 14, Wye Valley and Forest of Dean
Start Point:	Off A48, north of Newnham, GR 693120
Public Transport:	Gloucester-Lydney-Chepstow-Cardiff bus service stops in Newnham
Refreshments:	Newnham has three public houses and a fish and chip shop

The Blaize Bailey ridge offers a string of panoramic views over the Severn Estuary from its wooded heights. The walk starts and ends at the interesting little riverside town of Newnham, and much of the walk is over well waymarked paths.

From the car park on the very banks of the Severn head towards the town centre. At the prominent landmark of the clock tower turn up Station Road and continue over the railway. The lane bends to the right, and after the last house take a stile on the left. The path curves round the edge of the field before crossing a footbridge over Vostells Brook.

Over a lane bear to the right of the farm, down into a dip, and then go half left over a rise. At a stile into a belt of woodland go left, along what appears to be an ancient hollow way named Lumbars Lane. This joins a tarmac road, which should be briefly followed before ascending the rough ground ahead to join the Littledean road. You are now at Pleasant Stile, a wholly appropriate name when the estuarine views are contemplated.

Go right and then left behind the cottages. A gate ahead leads into a field, and the path now follows one side of the hedge, with a lane at the other side. This seemingly perverse arrangement allows the walker unobstructed views over the great languid loops of the Severn snaking sinuously below. The tower of Gloucester Cathedral and the line of the Cotswolds can also be seen on a clear day.

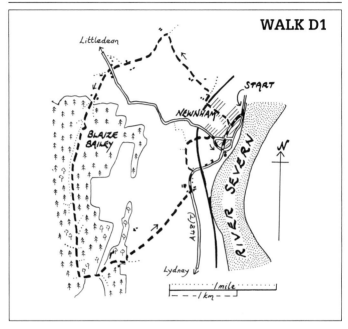

Briefly rejoin the lane, but branch right, enter the forest and go left (waymarked) to the viewpoint for another perspective of the estuary. Go up the steps to the rear, and follow the path to the left to rejoin the forestry drive in due course. Continue along the drive, but at the point it takes a sharp bend to the right continue ahead on a faint path. Now turn downhill at right angles, along the woodland edge.

Cross a stream and take the track leading half-left, towards a gate. The path now proceeds just inside the woodland fence to join a lane - go right (The Haie is on your left). A hollow way leads ahead, downhill to a gate, after which turn left. Pass over the portal of the first ever railway tunnel, now blocked, then over or through a wooden structure purporting to be a stile or gate. Bear half right over the spoil mound of the tunnel and cutting. Just to the left of the wood ahead is a stile of sorts. Now a sequence of gateways leads inexorably to the road. Go left (pavement), but carefully cross the road to a gateway where the road takes a sharp right-hand bend.

Follow the field edge round to the right, then go straight over the field to a stile, and then a gateway. Immediately to the right is another stile, and then half left is a bridge over the railway. Initially keep the field edge to your left, then veer right to the road, where go right.

Go right, on to The Green. A footpath follows the brow of the hill, looking over a little valley towards Blaize Bailey. Beneath your feet are vestigial remains of ancient earthworks. This little diversion ends up almost back on the A48, which must be crossed to reach the sanctuary of the churchyard. Whilst St Peter's is unashamedly Victorian, the view from a corner of the churchyard down on the river is almost vertiginous. A restful seat allows a lengthy appreciation, particularly on those dates when the Severn Bore is expected.

Return to the main street and walk downhill. Over the road the Victoria Hotel has a stained glass panel of 1622, depicting the "Grasshopper and the Ant". This is a reminder of the long history of the town. From here in 1171 Strongbow, Earl of Pembroke, set out to conquer Ireland. Later this became the "seaside" resort of the Forest of Dean.

At the bottom of the street is our starting point.

WALK D2:
Flaxley

Distance:	7km (4^{1}/$_{2}$m)
Map:	OS 1:25,000 Outdoor Leisure 14, Wye Valley and Forest of Dean
Start Point:	Collafield road, off Causeway Road, Cinderford, GR 666145
Public Transport:	Bus services from Parkend, Gloucester, Mitcheldean and Ross to the centre of Cinderford
Refreshments:	Royal Forester, Cinderford

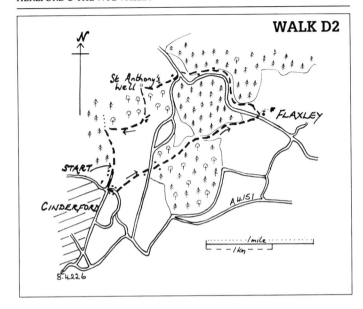

Vistas of the Severn Estuary, a former Cistercian Abbey, early industrial remains and a blessed spring to bathe in are all part of this walk. That these features are encapsulated in the hills and valleys of these Forest fringes is an added blessing.

Walk back along the Collafield road towards Cinderford. The view from the Royal Forester Inn is justifiably well known. From here the curves of the River Severn as it reluctantly meanders to the sea, are graphically portrayed.

Head down The Ruffits. A path funnels off at a triangle of grass on the left. Take a stile on the right, just before a kissing gate, and aim diagonally across the field. The path is in a groove, and continues obliquely downhill. Cross the minor road and follow the forest drive ahead. Go left at a junction.

Leave the woods and cross the narrow grassy field, but do not be tempted to enter the next wood. Instead go right, along the woodland edge. A sequence of stiles leads through orchards. At the corner of the woods continue ahead, slightly left, until on the brow of Pudding Hill the spire of Flaxley church and then the Abbey itself come into view.

The original Cistercian Abbey was founded in the mid-twelfth century by Roger, son of Milo, Earl of Hereford. Milo was allegedly killed on the spot whilst hunting. Unfortunately the building is not open to the public, for it incorporates parts of the original monastic buildings, including the fourteenth-century Abbot's Hall. There are extensive further extensions. At one time the occupant was Mrs Catherine Boevy, described as "The Perverse Widow" in Addison's story of Sir Roger de Coverley.

Now make for the church, to leave the field by a stile. Cross the road. The church of St Mary is another example of the prolific output of Sir George Gilbert Scott. This 1856 creation has a richly decorated interior which includes an inscription on the nave wall to Catherine Boevy, who is also remembered in Westminster Abbey.

Just down the drive to the Abbey and on the left is a stile into a field - the footplank points towards a bridge over the Westbury Brook, and on to the edge of Flaxley Woods, where go left. Recross the stream and continue just outside the wood. Go left at a farm drive, but then right again just before the road, again crossing the stream and swinging left. The Flaxley Valley once revelled in being the Vale of Castiard.

The path passes through the garden of a pair of cottages, and approaches Flaxley Mill. The house contains a fireback cast at the nearby forge in 1633, and the mill itself dates from around 1750. Go right, to enter the woodland opposite the mill, and join a forest track, where go left to the road. Turn briefly left and at the junction take the lane to the right. This passes derelict Guns Mill.

In the seventeenth century this area was a hive of industrial activity. A blast furnace was in operation by 1628. Cannon for the Civil War were made here. The furnace later became a paper mill. Continuing along the lane, the little stream clatters and chatters briefly alongside, freed from its labours of earlier centuries. Upper Mill is passed, once a fulling mill, again later a paper mill.

The track leads to the right to cross the stream. Just on your left is St Antony's Well, reputed to have healing properties, particularly for skin complaints.

With your back to the steps into the well, take the path now facing you. Now take a narrow path to the right, which leads above the waterworks, then turn off up a track opposite the waterworks house. Some mine levels are passed, then the path crosses the stream and climbs sharply. The quarries opposite display some steeply dipping beds.

Go left when the path joins a track. This leads through the woods, again with views over the Severn Vale, back to the start point.

WALK D3:
Soudley

Distance:	4km (2¹/₂m)
Map:	OS 1:25,000 Outdoor Leisure 14, Wye Valley and Forest of Dean
Start Point:	Soudley Upper Ponds, GR 662116
Public Transport:	Soudley is well served by buses from Lydney, Cinderford and Mitcheldean
Refreshments:	Dean Heritage Centre; pubs in Soudley
Other Information:	Forest of Dean Heritage Guides *Bradley Wood*, *Foundry Wood Forest Trail* and *Soudley Ponds* (from the Heritage Centre which opens daily)

The Dean Heritage Centre is a popular place which presents the history of the Forest in a very approachable manner. It also forms the hub of a number of wildlife walks encompassing hills, ponds and forest. This walk touches upon elements of those walks, in an area which is both interesting and attractive.

The car park lies at the access to the scenic drive to the Blaize Bailey ridge. Briefly follow this drive, then take the first forestry track to the right. This climbs steadily until a green-ringed post is seen on the right, marking the point to depart the track, the going now being more level. The path then rapidly descends down red sandstone crags, towards the final Soudley pond.

WALK D3

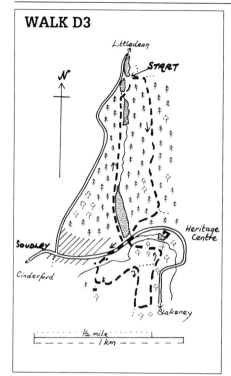

At the base of the slope go left to the road, then right. Take a lane on the left, crossing the disused railway line. Over a small stream and up the slope a path strikes off to the left, passing to the rear of the Zionist chapel of 1846. The path climbs amidst light woodland. Poisonous fungi such as the Death Cap and the Fly Agaric are to be found here - more cheerful are the nuthatches and tree-creepers which also frequent this area. A path leads off to the right, with views opening out over Soudley.

Cross a stile brandishing a lime green ring, on your left. The path now wends beneath low quarried outcrops, to which beech trees cling precariously, then curves off downhill, through bracken. At one point there is a seat looking down the valley towards Blakeney. Soon the path improves - turn right at the next junction, then left at the one after. The path overlooks the Heritage Centre. Once a mill that has seen a variety of uses, it now houses a museum of the Forest, featuring its industrial past.

One of the Centre's other attractions is the adventure playground which is passed as the path descends into the valley bottom. After crossing a stream turn right to join the road. Here go left and over the road is a path which will take you along the left-hand side of the ponds. They were originally thought to have been impounding ponds for the mill, but it has since been discovered that they were created about 150 years ago as fish ponds. Moorhens and mallard are the most common waterfowl to be seen, whilst in mid-summer dragonflies and damselflies are plentiful.

A motley collection of trees tower over the path, notably the western red cedars and the still taller Douglas firs. Whilst the first pond is open and normally a clear green the second is enclosed and brownish. Cross the dam to the third pond and turn left to return to the car park.

WALK D4:

Staple Edge and Mallards Pike

Distance:	8.5km (5¹/₂m)
Map:	OS 1:25,000 Outdoor Leisure 14, Wye Valley and Forest of Dean
Start Point:	Wench Ford Picnic Site, GR 654080
Public Transport:	Blakeney, 2km south of the start, is well served by buses from Gloucester and Chepstow, as well as more local services
Refreshments:	None, although at peak times an ice cream van appears at Wench Ford

Wench Ford is an open, attractive picnic spot with barbecue facilities, so on summer Sundays the air is thick with charcoal smoke. Nearby are some interesting industrial relics. This walk involves a climb to Staple Edge and back down to pretty Mallards Pike Lake, with more of those relics, and finally some long-distance views. Much of the route is on waymarked paths.

From the car park and public conveniences walk along the trackbed of the former Central Railway, in the opposite direction to Blakeney. Continue to the road, at the side of which is an exposed section of a "Roman" road - of some antiquity even if not of such distinguished origins. Continue along the road to the right, it is

186

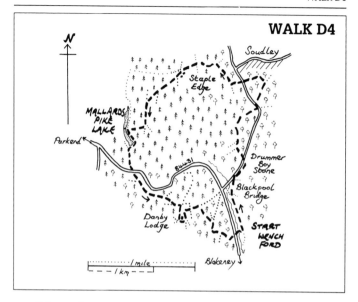

WALK D4

N

Soudley

Staple Edge

MALLARDS PIKE LAKE

Parkend

Drummer Boy Stone

Blackpool Bridge

Danby Lodge

START WENCH FORD

Blakeney

1 mile

1 km

possible to take a parallel path on the right, just inside the woods. A little further along, and just to the right of the road, is the Drummer Boy Stone. Of quartz conglomerate, it bears two hollows on the top, one of which contains some smelted iron. It is thought that it could even be an Iron Age furnace. Even the origin of the name is lost in the mists of time.

Cross the road and take the path up the slope. This crosses the forest track and climbs to another one. Here turn right and follow this track until it subsides to the road, opposite the Bradley Hill junction. Turn left along the main road, then take the path marked by a yellow arrow on the right. This leads towards a gate, but just beforehand another yellow arrow points to the left, and this is the route to follow. The next waymark to the left is even more easily missed, so take care.

Cross the road and up the rise join a track, where go right. The track climbs. Turn left at a junction, then cross a forestry track and climb a stile. The path passes the house on Staple Edge to join another track. Go left (ignore the sign to Mallards Pike) and then turn off to the right. At a left-handed bend continue bearing right to join a track. Turn left. Where this track joins another on a bend you should go over a stile on the right.

The path now takes you to Mallards Pike Lake, a pleasantly open expanse of water created by the Forestry Commission as recently as 1982, as a recreational amenity. Walk along the path to the left, cross the footbridge at the lake's outlet, and turn left, towards the road. Cross the road, bearing slightly left through a parking area and over a wooden barrier to a crossing path, where turn left.

Around here there is evidence of old mine and quarry workings, so take care and do not stray from the path. You may see the tall yellow flower spike of the great mullein on the waste ground. Keep to the right, uphill to a forestry track. Turn left, and when you see a red-ringed post on the left you should take the path on the right. This path swings round, at one point revealing views down the valley of the Blackpool Brook towards Blakeney. A little further along is the Jesus Rock, like many of these isolated boulders it is of quartz conglomerate, or puddingstone.

At the next junction turn right, climbing to another track by a free mine. It is unlikely to be operating, the coal being of poor quality. You are here by Danby Lodge, one of six lodges constructed following the reorganisation of the Forest during the reign of Charles II. They housed the Forest officials, each supervising an area of the Forest, or "Walk". Two of the lodges were badly damaged by rioters in 1688.

Turn left again, almost completing a circuit of the Lodge, then turn off right, downhill, and cross a track. Keep following the red-ringed posts right and right again by a pond. Now accompany this main forest track, turning left at one red-ringed post, then another, passing through an oak plantation. Cross the road to return to Wench Ford.

WALK D5:

New Fancy to Nagshead

Distance:	9km (5$^{1}/_{2}$m)
Map:	OS 1:25,000 Outdoor Leisure 14, Wye Valley and Forest of Dean
Start Point:	New Fancy picnic site, GR 628095
Public Transport:	Parkend to Cinderford bus service
Refreshments:	Rising Sun Inn, Moseley Green, pubs and cafe in Parkend.

That special blend of industrial past almost overtaken by robust nature that so typifies the Forest of Dean is well seen on this walk. From the New Fancy picnic site, once a colliery, to the former industrial centre of Parkend with its railway memories, and on to the Nagshead Nature Reserve, the walk finally passes a stone works and former impounding ponds. In few other areas is our industrial heritage so charmingly displayed.

New Fancy is the name of the colliery that once stood here. Once their imaginative names were their most attractive feature - "Speculation" and "Strip and At It" being other examples. New Fancy was operational between 1832 and 1944. Since 1961 a car park and picnic area have been created. The spoil heap has been partially retained, two thirds of it having been transported to form the foundations of steel works in South Wales. What remains has been sculpted to form a vantage point fit for a castle. From here miles of tree-clad valleys greet the eye.

Leave the site by the path that passes the public conveniences. Upon meeting a track go right to join the road. Go left to the junction, cross the road, and walk along the track ahead. Bear left at a Y junction. The track then curves right - at this point the Rising Sun Inn can be glimpsed for those needing an early detour. Next comes a choice of gates and stiles - opt for the gate straight in front of you and proceed to the Forestry Commission depot. Here go left to the road.

Turn right, downhill, but then turn left (signed to the church). St

Paul's was constructed in 1822 to an unusual octagonal plan in one of the choicest locations in the Forest. Now follow a sequence of white-ringed posts leading off opposite the church. Pass through the ash and beech woodland planted shortly before the building of the church. Plaques draw attention to exceptional specimens of each species.

The path curves to cross the northern extremity of the Dean Forest Railway, based at Norchard near Lydney. At the road go right, then left, to pass the Fountain Inn. On approaching the junction with the B4431 one sees on the right the King Edward VII limes, planted in 1902.

Go left at the junction to pass in front of the sawmill. Cross the road and walk alongside the mill to join the track to Nagshead. Stride towards the car park, opposite which a path leads to the part-time information centre. The Nagshead Nature Reserve of the Royal Society for the Protection of Birds was established in 1974. One might expect the birdlife to be rich and varied, and so it is - treecreepers, redstarts, hawfinches, nuthatches and pied flycatchers are just some of the species to be seen. Butterflies are also a feature

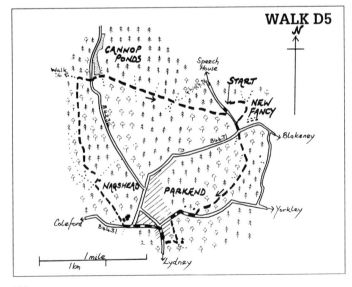

of the reserve, over thirty-five species being recorded. In addition to more common species grizzled and dingy skippers, holly blues, purple hairstreaks and marbled whites are to be found. The real stars are the white admiral and the silver-washed fritillary, which may be glimpsed in mid-summer.

Set off on the path signed for the Long and Short Nature Trails, marked by green ringed poles. This path passes over a stile and curves right, but we continue ahead at the point where the Trails branch acutely to the left.

The path drops to a forest drive (linking with Walk D4, going left here) where go right to the road. Cross over and pass to the left of the works where locally quarried Pennant sandstone is fashioned. Now cross the outlet to the Cannop Ponds, where a slippery water slide entrances children. The ponds themselves were created as storage reservoirs for the furnaces in Parkend.

Go very briefly left on a disused railway track, then follow the green-ringed posts to the right. There is a marked contrast between the densely packed conifers on the left and the open oak woodland where sheep graze to the right.

The path climbs. At a complicated little junction (again linking with Walk D4) we say goodbye to the green-ringed posts and go left, then immediately right. Continue climbing to reach the road. Now go left to see the picnic site entrance over the road.

WALK D6:
Cannop and Bixslade

Distance:	11km (7m)
Map:	OS 1:25,000 Outdoor Leisure 14, Wye Valley and Forest of Dean
Start Point:	Car park, Speech House Arboretum, GR 623122
Public Transport:	Parkend to Cinderford bus route
Refreshments:	Speech House Hotel
Other Information:	*Bixslade Forest Walk* leaflet (small charge)

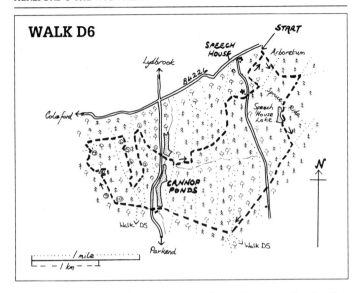

WALK D6

Although the Forest has many attractions, the network of paths, rides and tracks can be most confusing. Fortunately many waymarked routes have been developed, one, the Bixslade Forest Walk, forming part of this route. From the historic Speech House an arboretum, lakes and ponds, quarries and drift mines and some surprisingly open views are to be found.

A gate leads from the car park into the arboretum, which was founded in 1916. The trees are labelled, the dawn redwood being particularly interesting as the species was thought to be extinct until rediscovered in 1941. Continue through another gate and over a forestry track. The track we are now following bears left. Turn right at the next junction to pass through sombre plantations to another track. Cross over to find yourself on the banks of Speech House Lake, an ideal picnic spot. Most of the lakes and ponds in the Forest are connected with former industrial activity, but this one was created as recently as 1974, to increase wildlife interest.

Bear right, onto an earth dam, then left on a narrow path through the gorse thickets, then birch, to a forestry track. Turn right to reach the main road. Cross over and walk along another track until you come to an oblique crossing, where we continue ahead, downhill. The way is flanked by beech on one side and oak on the other. This brings you to a five way junction, at one corner of which stood the Three Brothers. These were tall oak trees, one of which has sadly perished. We take the second path to the right, now joining Walk D5. This leads straight downhill, possibly with fallow deer flitting about.

At the base of the slope jink right and left to cross a disused railway line and then a bridge over the outlet to the lowest of the Cannop Ponds. Continue past the stone works, specialities Bixhead Blue and Barnhill Grey sandstones, and cross the main road to join an old tramway. This climbs through the side valley of Bixslade, the old stone sleepers still discernible underfoot. An old sandstone quarry is seen on the right, just before a metal barrier has to be negotiated.

The tramway now bends right, still gaining height. On the left it passes a freeminer's coal mine, now used to drain the Spion Kop quarry above it. Detour right at a red-ringed post, then curving left. Yet more quarries in the Pennant Sandstone are seen to the right, and on the left is a viewpoint down Bixslade and towards the village of Yorkley.

Descend to the tramway and go right, to the next series of quarries, where go right, passing a disused crane, and with steep drops on either side. Ignore a track to the right and the first crossing track - although you are walking in the opposite direction from the recommended forest walk you should still be able to follow the red waymarks. Go right at the next track, then swiftly left. Cross two more forest tracks before curving to the right, through larch trees, then the holly understorey of the 1809 oak plantations.

Join another forestry track and go right, to a magnificent viewpoint - although recent plantations will eventually spoil the view. The Cannop Valley lies below, with the panorama from Ruardean Hill to Staple Edge further afield. Don't go right, but follow the path ahead to a tower from which a slightly different perspective is gained, albeit the near views are already obscured by fast-growing Douglas firs. Staple Edge can again be seen, also over Parkend towards Lydney and the village of Bream.

Now go right, then left, and left again along a path down through the woods to another forestry track. Left, then off the track to the right to another viewpoint, here looking over to the area known as Russell's Inclosure on the opposite flank of the Cannop Valley. There is one more forestry ride to cross before the road, at the other side of which is the outlet dam to the upper Cannop pond.

Cross the road to the car park and turn right, then bear left to the wooded parking area. From here a green-ringed post on the left stands at the entrance to the footpath we seek. This leads to a disused railway line, where we turn left. At the next junction turn right - there is a fading yellow arrow on a tree. Now climb back up the side of the valley, crossing another track.

As the next five-way junction take the second exit to the left, bearing right at the next two junctions to arrive at the road. Cross over, passing a car park, go over a stile and upon meeting a forestry track turn left towards a gate and another car park. To the right a path wends through the arboretum and back to the start.

WALK D7:

Castles and Caves

Distance:	5km (3m)
Map:	OS 1:25,000 Outdoor Leisure 14, Wye Valley and Forest of Dean
Start Point:	Clearwell Caves, GR 576082
Public Transport:	Scanty bus services from Gloucester, Chepstow and Coleford
Refreshments:	Tea shops at the Caves and Puzzle Wood, pubs in village

Clearwell is a village that has made a virtue of necessity. The ravages of iron-mining could so easily have left ugly, neglected scars, or have been landscaped into anonymity. Instead they have been nurtured, not merely out of academic interest, but as unique tourist attractions. This short walk links some of these intriguing sites, some agility being required if Puzzle Wood is visited.

Clearwell Caves provides a fascinating insight into the life of an iron ore miner. Expert guides, some ex-miners themselves, take visitors through eight large caverns which give the history of iron-ore working. It is a fascinating experience.

The return to daylight is somewhat sobering, but turn left (downhill) onto the road fronting the mine buildings, and proceed to a stile in the wall on the left, just before the tiny cemetery. The path continues along the side of a wood. Over two stiles, then right and follow the waymarks to emerge to the left of Platwell Farm.

Now turn right along the road (initially no footpath). Down the hill and on the left is the imposing entrance to Clearwell Castle. Built in Gothic style around 1730 by Thomas Wyndham, damaged by fire in 1929 and then ravaged internally by developers, it is now a country house hotel. By all means visit (in a paying capacity), but make sure your feet are clean!

Continue along the village street. The church of St Peter is in French Gothic style, built of local red sandstone with white Bath stone dressings. Flanked by funereal yews its appearance may be an acquired taste, but the interior of blue, red and white stone is

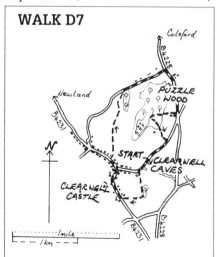

WALK D7

striking. Over the road the limestone of the village school is a cool contrast.

On the corner is a fourteenth-century cross. Follow the road to the left and a small detour to the left leads to a spring, with an inscription above which reads, "He sendeth the Springs into the Valleys which run among the Hills." Just to the right of the post office, take the footpath (signed).

Keep tight in to the quarry fence, cross a stile, then immediately on the right another stile. Follow the field edge to the left, and liberal yellow waymarks will lead you to Pingry Lane, where go right.

About half a mile of road walking leads to the busy B4228, where briefly go right to enter Puzzle Wood. Here the opencast iron workings were landscaped in the nineteenth century to form an oddly beautiful selection of walks.

Leave by the southern entrance, and follow the B4228 with a vestigial path on the verge, until just before the Lambsquay House Hotel, where a path along the field edge goes into Lambsquay Wood. Exit the wood, then go left to re-enter. This is a place far removed from the organised tourist world of the Caves and Puzzle Wood. Here the workings are unguarded, often overgrown, and at twilight little imagination is required to be disturbed by the eery atmosphere of this grotesque landscape, where tree roots seem locked in grim combat with rock outcrops.

Exiting the wood, cross the field diagonally, over a stile, then follow the field edge to the road, passing a locked air shaft. Turn right to return to the start.

WALK D8:
Rocks and stones

Distance:	5.5km (3¹/₂m)
Map:	OS 1:25,000 Outdoor Leisure 14, Wye Valley and Forest of Dean
Start Point:	Staunton Church GR 551126
Public Transport:	Bus service from Monmouth and Coleford, also Lydney and a rare Gloucester service.
Refreshments:	White Horse Inn, Staunton

Lurking amongst the luxuriant woodlands of Highmeadow Woods, where the north-eastern boundary of the Forest of Dean is formed by the River Wye, are some real monsters! These are the massive boulders known as the Suck Stone, the Buck Stone and Near

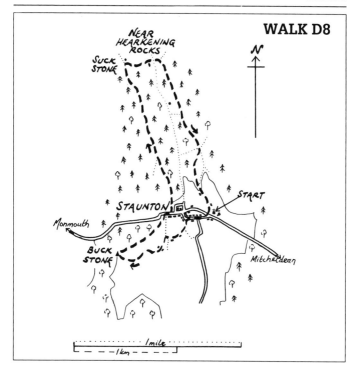

Hearkening Rocks. Fortunately they are quite harmless (except to those who are over-ambitious in clambering over them), and are easy to track down because they are relatively motionless.

The earliest parts of the church are the twelfth-century tower and north arcade, but the eleventh-century font, a cube of endearing simplicity, is of more interest. Also of note is the stone pulpit, of around 1500, which is accessed via the stairs to the central tower.

Cross the A4136 and walk down the road opposite, a far cry from those unfortunate properties lining the busy main road. Pass the junction with the Newland and Redbrook road but at a sharp right hand bend continue ahead, along a lane. Follow this lane as it curves left then right, and at the next junction go first right then left.

Views open out over the Wye Valley to the south as height is gained. After "Assisi" take the track curving to the right to the Buck Stone. This is a massive boulder of quartz conglomerate to which a host of legends cling. It was a logan, or rocking stone, until Victorian vandals rolled it down the hill in 1885. It is now firmly cemented into place. Supposedly it rocked at the approach of sinners. Alternatively it was an ancient British look-out post, and the rocking could be heard in the valley below. If you walk around it three times your wish should be granted - mine wasn't!

At 279m (915ft) this is one of the highest points in the Forest of Dean, with correspondingly fine views. The path continues along the ridge before descending temptingly close to the White Horse Inn, which proudly proclaims itself to be the first and last pub in England. This is true so far as the A4136 is concerned.

Fifty metres west of the White Horse Inn an alleyway alongside High View is waymarked into Highmeadow Woods. The path descends, somewhat damply, to join a forestry track. Turn right and follow the track. Clear-felling has opened out views in places, relieving the oppressiveness of the conifer plantation.

Look out for a waymark on the right, for above the track is the Suck Stone, from this side looking rather like a beached whale. Walk right round, as a true impression of its size is only gained from the dark side. It is supposedly the largest detached boulder in the country - estimates of its weight range from 4,000 to 14,000 tons.

The path (still waymarked) continues to the right of the Suck Stone, shortly to arrive at Near Hearkening Rocks. The name is said to derive from the ability of the rocks to amplify sounds in the forest, assisting keepers in days gone by to detect poachers. From the top of the rocks, where trees cling by contorted roots, there are fine views into Wales.

The path continues to the rear, leading once more into the forest. Cross a forestry track onto another path. Bear right at the next junction onto a better path. There are views to the left over a young plantation to Coppet Hill, Symonds Yat and Christchurch. You then come to a complex little junction of five paths, where bear half right, uphill through a newly planted area. Don't cross the stile, but bear left, to join a track leading to the right, past a few houses and so to the church.

WALK D9:
Speech House and the Sculpture Trail

Distance:	6.5km (4m)
Map:	OS 1:25,000 Outdoor Leisure 14, Wye Valley and Forest of Dean
Start Point:	Lay-by opposite Pedalbikeaway on Lydbrook to Parkend road, GR 609124
Public Transport:	Parkend to Cinderford bus service passes Speech House
Refreshments:	Speech House Hotel
Other Information:	Forestry Commission *Sculpture Trail Walk* leaflet, small charge

The Forestry Commission has over recent years actively developed the Forest of Dean as a recreational resource. This has not been limited to conventional picnic sites and waymarked routes. One of the most imaginative innovations has been the Sculpture Trail, a route visiting a number of strategically placed features - not to be confused with the museum pieces of classical style. These are modern works by selected artists. Some pieces harmonise with their environment, others startle with incongruous ingenuity. Most of this walk follows the waymarked route.

From the lay-by walk south and go up an embankment on the left to join a disused railway line, curving right. At the second green-ringed marker post scramble up the bank to another former line, where go left. Green woodpeckers and jays flit around amongst the oaks and silver birch on either side of the slightly elevated trackbed.

Once over a second stile a small detour to the left reveals the first sculptures. The Black Dome of 900 charred larch logs, and then the Fire and Water Boats, also charred and now biodegrading. Return to the railway track (the Sculpture Trail has blue waymarks). A long straight now follows. This was one of the main railway lines through the Forest, from Lydney to Cinderford. It is appropriate that we now pass the Iron Road, at first glance just twenty railway

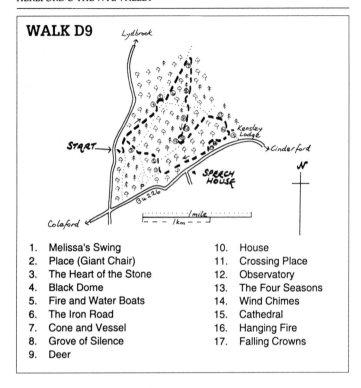

WALK D9

Lydbrook

START →

Kensley Lodge

→ Cinderford

SPEECH HOUSE

B4226

Coleford ←

1 mile
1 km

1. Melissa's Swing
2. Place (Giant Chair)
3. The Heart of the Stone
4. Black Dome
5. Fire and Water Boats
6. The Iron Road
7. Cone and Vessel
8. Grove of Silence
9. Deer
10. House
11. Crossing Place
12. Observatory
13. The Four Seasons
14. Wind Chimes
15. Cathedral
16. Hanging Fire
17. Falling Crowns

sleepers, but each is incised with a carving, such as a feather or a factory. The Lydbrook line joined along here, at Serridge junction.

A blue waymarked stile on the right leads to the next sculptures, the Cone and Vessel - realistic except in their gargantuan size. The pine cone and the acorn cup appear to have fallen from the trees above. The path loops round, passing the Grove of Silence - perhaps these plaques are a little too obscure. Soon afterwards take a path to the left, crossing another path and then bearing right and left to pass seven deer, worthy of more than a glance to identify some of the detailed motifs on these highly original interpretations.

The path now passes House, a tall metal tower, before skirting a pond being crossed by a herd of deer. These most effective

Sculpture Trail - Deer

Sculpture Trail - Cathedral Window

representations are made of wire, now rusted to a suitable colour. Around the other side of the pond is a staircase, providing a viewpoint worthy of the name, Observatory.

Another straight stretch follows, then a steep right turn at a crossing. A detour to the left reveals the Four Seasons, now reverting to nature. A gate leads to the precincts of Kensley Lodge. The path curves round to one of the most accessible of the sculptures, the Cathedral Window. This massive stained glass creation is suspended over the path, and is highly impressive, especially when backlit by the sun. Nearby you may hear the wind chimes.

The broad path now leads towards a car park, but turn right immediately before it. High above on the right is a massive cast iron crown - Hanging Fire. You could follow the path around to the left to see eight smaller crowns in a tree, but if so return to and continue along the original path to another car park. Soon the Speech House is seen on the left. Once the administrative headquarters of the Forest, it was built of local stone between 1678 and 1680. It used to be known as the King's Lodge, the Verderer's Court which was held here protected both the Royal prerogative and local privileges. It is now a Trust House Hotel.

Opposite the Speech House are the King Edward VII yews, a clump of trees planted to commemorate the coronation of 1902. Bear left towards the railed Sanzen-Barker oak, planted in 1810 it was named after a Deputy Surveyor of the Forest, who developed visitor facilities between 1954 and 1968.

Now keep to the right, following blue-ringed posts, to find Melissa's Swing, which proves irresistible to most visitors (not just children). Next is the gigantic chair frame of Place, overlooking the Cannop Valley, a marvellously evocative spot. From here the path swings round, still following the waymarks, to find the Heart of the Stone. Like a fish leaping out of the rough hewn stones, its positioning over the former Rose in Hand coal mine could symbolise the new recreational life of the Forest, springing from it's industrial past. Continue on from here (not now on the waymarked route). Cross the disused railway line to return to the road, where go left for about 250m to find the start point.

WALK D10:

Ruardean Hill

Distance:	9km (5¹/₂m)
Map:	OS 1:25,000 Outdoor Leisure 14, Wye Valley and Forest of Dean
Start Point:	Car park, Drybrook, GR 645174
Public Transport:	Gloucester to Cinderford bus service
Refreshments:	Pubs in Drybrook and Ruardean

On the northern rim of the Forest of Dean the woods part to reveal wide-ranging views, and also the scarred terrain of former industry. Off the beaten tourist track, there is more than a hint of walking through people's backyards, but the intrepid reader of this book will find the alternation of attractive countryside and industry reverting to wildlife no less interesting for all that. Careful routefinding is required amidst a myriad of tracks.

From the car park turn left along the main street of Drybrook, and turn left along Varnister Lane. It is possible to detour slightly along Whitehill Lane to avoid some of the traffic on this narrow road. Turn right at the second footpath sign on the right, over a stile by the entrance to abandoned White Hill Farm.

There is another stile in the top corner of the field, leading to a green lane. From here there are glimpses into the depths of the large limestone quarry. At the next stile there are views over Hope Mansell to Penyard, but we turn left, following the fieldside through gateways and over stiles. At an old cottage cross a track to a stile, then bear half left to the hedge ahead. Go left and follow this hedge as it curves round to a rough log stile.

Keep ahead, over two individualistic metal stiles, to arrive at a road. Cross over and walk along Varnister Lane (a different one), joining the B4227 through Ruardean. This ordinary little village has an eyecatching church - the tall, buttressed spire can be seen for miles. It also has a tympanum of St George slaying the dragon, which is another outstanding example of the twelfth-century

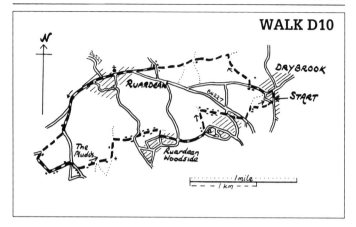

Herefordshire School of sculpture. Continue along the road signed to Joys Green and The Pludds. On the outskirts of the village is a seat overlooking the great incised valley of the River Wye.

Turn left towards The Pludds, passing an old mine, then turn right along a green lane. From a gateway near the entrance to this lane is an even better view over the Wye as it loops around Coppet Hill, from Kerne Bridge towards Welsh Bicknor. The lane emerges on a metalled road, which should be followed as it curves around to the left. Now there is a different view, of the Forest of Dean as it rolls away to the south.

Join Eddy's Lane at prosaic The Pludds. Turn right, and then take a track opposite the telephone kiosk, through bracken and gorse. This joins a lane - go left, climbing, to a tarmac road. Keep left here, until the tarmac ends. Now fork right, curving downhill to join another tarmac lane, but branch immediately to the left, dropping towards the head of a valley. Climb out onto another lane, and cross Meend Lane to Bakers Piece Lane.

At the end of this narrow lane escape to the right on a path which rises to Farm Road, where turn left. Go over the crossroads, signed to Drybrook. This simple road walking comes to an end at an assemblage of objects - a reservoir, a triangulation column and a flagpole, so you should be in no doubt that this is Ruardean Hill. This is the point to turn left, at the side of a house, just after a junction.

The track passes a beacon, with bell heather around, and then descends slightly to bend right. Do not be deflected by other tracks. Continue ahead at a junction onto Betts Lane (the Nelson Arms is just to the left). Turn left along a lane immediately after the first house on the left, pass through a kissing gate, and then turn right through the yard of Ground Farm. Cross the disused railway line to join Quabbs Lane by the school. Turn right, then left, to return to the start.

Mistletoe

APPENDIX 1: LONGER DISTANCE PATHS

OFFA'S DYKE PATH

King Offa ruled Mercia between AD 757 and 796. A formidable monarch, he developed diplomacy, notably with the Pope and Charlemagne, and introduced the penny into our currency. For many years prior to his rule Mercia had been expanding towards and into Wales, resulting in counter-offensives and reversals. After Offa's accession there was a great battle at Hereford in 760, with further battles later in his reign.

The building of the Dyke is first recorded about 100 years after its completion, but there is little doubt that Offa was the only ruler of sufficient stature in those dark days to be able to command its construction. Why it should be built remains a matter of some conjecture. Some have argued that it was simply to mark the border between Mercia and Wales. Others consider that it must have had a defensive role - even today the depth of the ditch and the height of the ramparts are in some places quite formidable. The Dyke is usually strategically placed on west facing slopes, and it has been suggested that it was topped by a wooden palisade. It was certainly a massive undertaking - it has been estimated that the ditching and ramparting would have taken about 4 million man hours.

The actual route of the Dyke over much of its length remains obscure. Between Chepstow and Monmouth there are clear remains, as there are between Kington and just to the north of Montgomery. Again, near Oswestry there is enough to identify the route, but elsewhere little or nothing can be discerned. Perhaps a Dyke was not required along the complete length because of the presence of friendly peoples, or because the terrain was impenetrable.

The Offa's Dyke Path, the result of extensive work by the Offa's Dyke Association, was finally officially opened by the Countryside Commission in 1971. The path does not faithfully follow the line of the Dyke itself, deserting it for more scenic delights, notably between Monmouth and Kington, and in the very north of its 270km (168 miles). The path runs from Sedbury (to the south of Chepstow) to Monmouth, then along the Monnow Valley to join the eastern extremity of the Black Mountains. It then runs to Hay-on-Wye,

Kington, Knighton, Montgomery and thence to Prestatyn on the coast of North Wales.

A number of walks in this book use lengths of the Path: A6 and A7 near Kington, A9 on the Black Mountains, A14 in the Monnow Valley (on the Three Castles alternative), C10 near Monmouth, C11 (Redbrook and Newland), C12 (Tintern), C14 (Brockweir to Bigsweir) and C16 (Wintour's Leap).

Particularly in the Wye Valley south of Monmouth it is easily possible to work out longer circular routes using the above walks and/or lengths of the Wye Valley Walk on the opposite bank.

WYE VALLEY WALK

This Walk is a far more recent creation, its only rationale being that it never strays far from the River Wye - sufficient justification for most people. The Walk heads from Chepstow to Ross, and thence to Hereford and Hay-on-Wye. It then continues into Wales, to Builth Wells and Rhyader - 126km (78 miles) are in England.

Again, a number of walks in this book utilise the well-waymarked Wye Valley Walk. These are: A12 (Monnington-on-Wye), A20 (Hereford), C1 (Haugh Wood), C4 (Fownhope), C6 (Ross-on-Wye), C7 (Coppet Hill), C8 (Symonds Yat), C13 (The Narth) and C17 (Wynd Cliff).

LINKED WALKS

Some of the walks in this book link directly, even overlap with others on occasion. In other cases they are but a short distance apart, and a link can easily be forged.

The main opportunities to link walks are:

A1	(Richard's Castle and High Vinnals) and A2 (Bringewood Forge and Downton Castle)
A6	(Hergest Ridge) and A7 (On Offa's Dyke)
A17	(Bringsty Common) and A18 (By River Teme and Sapey Brook)
A8	(Merbach Hill and Arthur's Stone) and A10 (Vagar Hill)
B1	(Malvern Town) and B2 (Worcestershire Beacon)
B2	(Worcestershire Beacon) and B4 (The Central Ridge)
B4	(The Central Ridge) and B5 (Herefordshire Beacon)

C9 (Buckholt Wood and Welsh Newton Common) and C10
    (Monmouth and The Kymin)
C12 (Tintern Abbey and the Devil's Pulpit) and C14
    (Brockweir to Bigsweir)
C16 (Wintour's Leap) and C17 (Wynd Cliff)
D3 (Soudley) and D5 (New Fancy to Nagshead)
D3 (Soudley) and D6 (Cannop and Bixslade)
D5 (New Fancy to Nagshead) and D6 (Cannop and Bixslade)

APPENDIX 2: PUBLIC TRANSPORT

RAIL

Hereford stands at the junction of the county's limited rail services.
Lines from London Paddington and Birmingham (New Street at
present) converge on Worcester, and then run to Malvern Link,
Great Malvern, Colwall, Ledbury and so to Hereford. From Crewe
and Shrewsbury comes another line, with intermediate stations at
Ludlow and Leominster. A line then leads to Abergavenny and
South Wales.

Gloucester is another focal point, this time for services along the
north bank of the Severn Estuary to Cardiff. There are stations at
Lydney and Chepstow.

Enquiries   - Birmingham   021 643 2711
               - Gloucester   0452 529501
               - Shrewsbury   0743 364041

BUS

Hereford acts as the hub of services to the other towns of the county,
with limited services to the villages lying off the main roads. Great
Malvern is largely served from Worcester.

Hereford and Worcester County Council produces a map of
services and leaflets based on the towns giving detailed timetables.
Changes to services and times are frequent. The map (free) and
timetable leaflets (15p each at the time of writing) are available
from:

County Engineer and Planning Officer,
Hereford and Worcester County Council
County Hall, Spetchley Road,
Worcester WR5 2NP Tel: 0905 766800

Gloucestershire and Gwent County Councils produce information for their respective areas, to the east and west of the Wye respectively. Contact addresses are given in Appendix 3.

Alternatively check with the local tourist information centres, again, listed in Appendix 3.

APPENDIX 3: USEFUL ADDRESSES

FOOTPATH AUTHORITIES

Gloucestershire County Council - The County Surveyor, Shire Hall, Gloucester, GL1 2TH

Gwent County Council - The County Planning Officer, County Hall, Cwmbran, NP44 2XF

Hereford and Worcester County Council - County Engineer & Planning Officer, County Hall, Spetchley Road, Worcester WR5 2NP

Shropshire County Council - Chief Recreational Services Officer, Winston Churchill Building, Redbrook Centre, Redbrook Road, Shrewsbury, SY3 9BJ

TOURIST INFORMATION CENTRES

Bromyard -	Council Offices, 1 Rowberry Street. 0885 482341
Chepstow -	The Gate House, High Street. 02912 3772
Cinderford -	The Library, Belle Vue Road. 0594 822581
Coleford -	The Market Place. 0594 36307
Hereford -	Town Hall, St Owens Street. 0432 268430
Kington -	Council Offices, 2 Mill Street. 0544 230202
Ledbury -	Church Lane. 0531 6147
Leominster -	6 School Lane. 0568 616460
Ludlow -	Castle Street. 0584 875053
Malvern -	The Winter Gardens, Grange Road. 0684 892700
Monmouth -	The Shirehall (seasonal). 0600 713899

Ross-on-Wye - 20 Broad Street. 0989 62768
Tintern -   Tintern Abbey (seasonal). 0291 689431

OTHER ORGANISATIONS

Cadw (Welsh Historic Monuments), Brunel House, 2 Fitzalan Road,
    Cardiff, CF2 1UY
Campaign for the Preservation of Rural England, 4 Hobart Place,
    London, SW1W OHY
Countryside Commission, John Dower Hose, Crescent Place,
    Cheltenham, Glos, GL50 3RA
English Heritage, Fortress House, Savile Row, London, W1X 2HE
The Forestry Commission, Marches Forest District, Whitcliffe,
    Ludlow, Shropshire, SY8 2HD
The Forestry Commission, West England Conservancy and Dean
    Surveyorship, Crown Offices, Bank Street, Coleford, Glos,
    GL16 8BA
Herefordshire Nature Trust Ltd, 25 Castle Street, Hereford,
    HR1 2NW
National Trust, Severn Regional Office, Mythe End House,
    Tewkesbury, Glos, GL20 6GB
Nature Conservancy Council (West Midlands Region), Attingham
    Park, Shrewsbury, SY4 4TW
Offa's Dyke Association, West Street, Knighton, Powys, LD7 1EW
The Ramblers' Association, 1/5 Wandsworth Road, London,
    SW8 2XX
Royal Society for the Protection of Birds, The Lodge, Sandy, Beds,
    SG19 2DL
The Youth Hostels Association, Trevelyan House, 8 St Stephen's
    Hill, St Albans, Herts, AL1 2DY

USEFUL BOOKS

HEREFORDSHIRE

British Regional Geology: The Welsh Borderland, 3rd edn, NERC/
    Institute of Geological Science, HMSO 1971
Bromyard & District Local History Society, *A Pocketful of Hops*, 1989
R.Christiansen, *Forgotten Railways, Vol.II Severn Valley & Welsh*

Borders, David and Charles 1988

Herefordshire Federation of Women's Institutes, *The Herefordshire Village Book*, Countryside Books/HFWI 1989

C.Hopkinson, *Herefordshire Under Arms*, Bromyard & District Local History Society

N.Howes, *Herefordshire Curiosities*, ARCH 1990

A.Johnson & S.Punter, *Aspects of Herefordshire*, Logaston Press 1987

K.Lawrence-Smith, *Tales of Old Herefordshire*, Countryside Books 1990

C.A.Lewis (ed), *The Glaciations of Wales and Adjoining Regions*, Longman 1970

J.Minton, *Access to the Herefordshire Countryside Today*, Minton & Minton 1989

N.Pevsner, *The Buildings of England: Herefordshire*, Penguin 1963

Mike Salter, *The Castles of Herefordshire & Worcestershire*, Folly 1989

Mike Salter, *The Old Parish Churches of Herefordshire*, Folly 1990

J.W.Tonkin, *Herefordshire*, Batsford 1977

A.Watkins, *The Old Straight Track*, Abacus 1974

John & Margaret West, *A History of Herefordshire*, Phillimore 1985

Woolhope Naturalists Field Club, *Herefordshire*, British Publishing Co. 1951

MALVERN HILLS

W.Dreghorn, *Geology Explained in the Severn Vale and Cotswolds*, David and Charles 1967

G.H.Green & B.Westwood, *The Nature of Worcestershire*, Barracuda 1991

P.Hurle, *The Malvern Hills*, Phillimore 1984

Nature Conservancy Council, *Malvern Hills - A Students Guide to the Geology*, NCC 1989

C.Moody, *The Silhouette of Malvern*, Priory Press 1953

B.S.Smith, *A History of Malvern*, Alan Sutton & The Malvern Bookshop, 1978

S.C.Stanford, *The Malvern Hillforts*, L.Tilley & Son 1973

V.Waite, *Malvern Country*, Phillimore 1979

WYE VALLEY AND FOREST OF DEAN

Forestry Commission, *Dean Forest and Wye Valley*, HMSO 1974

W.Dreghorn, *Geology Explained in the Forest of Dean and Wye Valley*, David & Charles 1968

Forest of Dean and Wye Valley, AA/Ordnance Survey 1988

E.J.Mason, *The Wye Valley*, Hale 1987

M.H.Morris, *Reflections of Ross-on-Wye*, Published by author 1973

H.W.Paar, *An Industrial Tour of the Wye Valley and Forest of Dean*, West London Archaeological Society Publications Committee 1980

R.Sale, *The Wye Valley*, Wildwood 1984

M.Salter, *Parish Churches of the Forest of Dean*, Folly Publications 1990

D.Verey, *Gloucestershire: The Vale and Forest of Dean*, Penguin 1970

OFFA'S DYKE PATH

E.& K.Kay & M.Richards, *Offa's Dyke Path - South*, Aurum Press 1989

M.Richards, *Through Welsh Border Country*, Thornhill 1976

C.Wright, *A Guide to Offa's Dyke Path*, Constable 1986

WYE VALLEY WALK

D.Hunter, *Wye Valley Walk*, Cicerone Press 1992

CICERONE GUIDES

Cicerone publish a wide range of reliable guides to walking and climbing in Britain, and other general interest books.

LAKE DISTRICT - General Books
A DREAM OF EDEN
LAKELAND VILLAGES
LAKELAND TOWNS
REFLECTIONS ON THE LAKES
OUR CUMBRIA
THE HIGH FELLS OF LAKELAND
CONISTON COPPER A History
LAKELAND - A taste to remember (Recipes)
THE LOST RESORT?
CHRONICLES OF MILNTHORPE
LOST LANCASHIRE
THE PRIORY OF CARTMEL

LAKE DISTRICT - Guide Books
CASTLES IN CUMBRIA
THE CUMBRIA CYCLE WAY
WESTMORLAND HERITAGE WALK
IN SEARCH OF WESTMORLAND
CONISTON COPPER MINES Field Guide
SCRAMBLES IN THE LAKE DISTRICT
MORE SCRAMBLES IN THE LAKE DISTRICT
WINTER CLIMBS IN THE LAKE DISTRICT
WALKS IN SILVERDALE/ARNSIDE
BIRDS OF MORECAMBE BAY
THE EDEN WAY
WALKING ROUND THE LAKES

NORTHERN ENGLAND (outside the Lakes
BIRDWATCHING ON MERSEYSIDE
CANOEISTS GUIDE TO THE NORTH EAST
THE CLEVELAND WAY & MISSING LINK
THE DALES WAY
DOUGLAS VALLEY WAY
HADRIANS WALL Vol 1 The Wall Walk
HERITAGE TRAILS IN NW ENGLAND
THE ISLE OF MAN COASTAL PATH
THE LANCASTER CANAL
LAUGHS ALONG THE PENNINE WAY
A NORTHERN COAST-TO-COAST
NORTH YORK MOORS Walks
THE REIVERS WAY (Northumberland)
THE RIBBLE WAY
ROCK CLIMBS LANCASHIRE & NW
THE YORKSHIRE DALES A walker's guide
WALKING IN THE SOUTH PENNINES
WALKING IN THE NORTH PENNINES
WALKS IN THE YORKSHIRE DALES (3 VOL)
WALKS IN LANCASHIRE WITCH COUNTRY
WALKS TO YORKSHIRE WATERFALLS (2 vol)
WALKS ON THE WEST PENNINE MOORS
WALKING NORTHERN RAILWAYS EAST
WALKING NORTHERN RAILWAYS WEST

DERBYSHIRE & EAST MIDLANDS
WHITE PEAK WALKS - 2 Vols
HIGH PEAK WALKS
WHITE PEAK WAY
KINDER LOG

THE VIKING WAY
THE DEVIL'S MILL (Novel)
WHISTLING CLOUGH (Novel)
WALES & WEST MIDLANDS
THE RIDGES OF SNOWDONIA
HILLWALKING IN SNOWDONIA
HILL WALKING IN WALES (2 Vols)
ASCENT OF SNOWDON
WELSH WINTER CLIMBS
SNOWDONIA WHITE WATER SEA & SURF
SCRAMBLES IN SNOWDONIA
SARN HELEN Walking Roman Road
ROCK CLIMBS IN WEST MIDLANDS
THE SHROPSHIRE HILLS A Walker's Guide
HEREFORD & THE WYE VALLEY A Walker's Guide
THE WYE VALLEY WALK

SOUTH & SOUTH WEST ENGLAND
COTSWOLD WAY
EXMOOR & THE QUANTOCKS
THE KENNET & AVON WALK
THE SOUTHERN-COAST-TO-COAST
SOUTH DOWNS WAY & DOWNS LINK
SOUTH WEST WAY - 2 Vol
WALKING IN THE CHILTERNS
WALKING ON DARTMOOR
WALKERS GUIDE TO DARTMOOR PUBS
WALKS IN KENT
THE WEALDWAY & VANGUARD WAY

SCOTLAND
THE BORDER COUNTRY - WALKERS GUIDE
SCRAMBLES IN LOCHABER
SCRAMBLES IN SKYE
THE ISLAND OF RHUM
CAIRNGORMS WINTER CLIMBS
THE CAIRNGORM GLENS (Mountainbike Guide)
THE ATHOLL GLENS (Mountainbike Guide)
WINTER CLIMBS BEN NEVIS & GLENCOE
SCOTTISH RAILWAY WALKS
TORRIDON A Walker's Guide
SKI TOURING IN SCOTLAND

REGIONAL BOOKS UK & IRELAND
THE MOUNTAINS OF ENGLAND & WALES
VOL 1 WALES
VOL 2 ENGLAND
THE MOUNTAINS OF IRELAND
THE ALTERNATIVE PENNINE WAY
THE RELATIVE HILLS OF BRITAIN
LIMESTONE - 100 BEST CLIMBS

Also a full range of EUROPEAN and OVER-SEAS guidebooks - walking, long distance trails, scrambling, ice-climbing, rock climbing.

Other guides are constantly being added to the Cicerone List.
Available from bookshops, outdoor equipment shops or direct (send s.a.e. for price list) from
CICERONE, 2 POLICE SQUARE, MILNTHORPE, CUMBRIA, LA7 7PY